Reading Group Choices
2 0 0 9

READING GROUP *Choices*

℘elebrating
15 years
of selecting
books for
lively discussions.

For further information, contact:
Barbara Drummond Mead
Reading Group Choices
532 Cross Creek Court
Chester, MD 21619
Toll-free: 1-866-643-6883
info@ReadingGroupChoices.com
www.ReadingGroupChoices.com

Welcome to READING GROUP Choices

It is such a happiness when good people
get together—and they always do.
—Jane Austen, Emma

As we celebrate the 15th anniversary of *Reading Group Choices*, we honor reading groups, book clubs, readers' circles and, indeed, any gathering whose members share the joy of reading and literary conversation. In this age of text messaging, blogging, and cell phone conversations, it is refreshing to discover that there are so many of you who still find pleasure, adventure, knowledge, self awareness, and even solace between the covers of a book and who enjoy the company of those who share your love of reading. October is National Reading Group Month, a tribute to the continuing growth of these groups that offer the opportunity for discussion and a real exchange of ideas.

Reading Group Choices 2009 selections continue to incorporate your ideas and suggestions for discussible books. In this edition, you will find many literary choices: mystery; memoir; historical fiction; current affairs; humor and literary fiction. Something to meet almost every taste. We hope that you will find our suggestions helpful in planning your book club year.

Here's to another great year of friendship and discussion! We look forward to another 15 years of sharing our selections and receiving your thoughts.

And, thanks for keeping the joy of reading alive.

—Barbara and Charlie Mead

Author Conversations are Easy and Fun!

All your group needs is to read the book, have a speaker phone, and let the chat begin!

Tips for a successful author conversations:

- Schedule a **Reading Group Choices'** author by registering at www.ReadingGroupChoices.com
- Have your group read the book – ***very important.***
- Meet at least 30 minutes before the conversation to prepare questions for the author. Use questions from *Reading Group Choices* and other sources, as well as your own.
- Have an order of questions to prevent two or more people talking at once (very confusing for the author).
- Have everyone get a chance to speak to avoid one member dominating the conversation.
- Have members say their first names before asking a question of the author; this gives the author a feeling of personal connection even though the chat is on the phone.

Have a fun and lively conversation!

CONTENTS

Early in 2008, we asked thousands of book groups to tell us what books they read and discussed during the previous year that they enjoyed most. The top ten titles were:

1. **Water for Elephants**, *by Sara Gruen*

2. **The Glass Castle**, *by Jeannette Walls*

3. **Snow Flower and the Secret Fan**, *by Lisa See*

4. **A Thousand Splendid Suns**, *by Khaled Hosseini*

5. **The Memory Keeper's Daughter**, *by Kim Edwards*

6. (tie) **Eat, Pray, Love**, *by Elizabeth Gilbert*

6. (tie) **The Kite Runner**, *by Khaled Hosseini*

7. **My Sister's Keeper**, *by Jodi Picoult*

8. **Nineteen Minutes**, *by Jodi Picoult*

9. **The Book Thief**, *by Markus Zusak*

10. **Three Cups of Tea**, *by Greg Mortenson and David Oliver Relin*

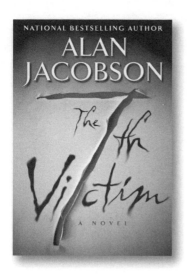

THE 7TH VICTIM

AUTHOR: **Alan Jacobson**

PUBLISHER: Vanguard Press, September 2008

WEBSITE: www.vanguardpressbooks.com
www.the7thvictimthebook.com

AVAILABLE IN:
Hardcover, 420 pages $25.95
ISBN: 978-1-593-15494-3

SUBJECT: Intrigue/Women's Lives/Suspense
(Fiction)

"Alan Jacobson is a hell of a writer, and his lead character, Karen Vail, is a hell of a lady: tough, smart, funny, and very believable. The 7th Victim is an impressively researched novel about serial murder packed into a tightly twisting plot. Very scary, and very good. This reads like a Nelson DeMille book. And I should know." —**Nelson DeMille,** *New York Times* **bestselling author of** *Wild Fire*

SUMMARY: The Dead Eyes killer lurks in the backyard of the FBI's famed Behavioral Analysis Unit. His brutal murders, unlike any others previously encountered, confound the local task force, despite the gifted skills of Special Agent Karen Vail, the first female ever promoted to the profiling unit. As the Dead Eyes killer grows bolder, Vail discovers that the seventh victim holds the key to all that stirs this killer . . . the key that will unlock secrets. Secrets that threaten to destroy her, that could bring down her storied and promising career.

The 7th Victim is a terrifying and memorable work of psychological suspense, with rich, believable characters and a chilling, intricate plot that will keep you guessing until the end.

ABOUT THE AUTHOR: **Alan Jacobson** is the bestselling author of the critically acclaimed thrillers *False Accusations* and *The Hunted*. Alan has a degree in English and a doctorate in chiropractic medicine. He achieved prominence as an Agreed Medical Examiner and was subsequently appointed to the position of Qualified Medical Evaluator by the state of California.

1. Based on what you learned about behavioral analysis (profiling), do you feel it is a valuable law enforcement tool for helping to catch serial offenders?

2. Were you emotionally engaged in the characters—did you care what happened to Vail? To Jonathan? To Robby and Bledsoe?

3. What was your favorite scene?

4. Describe your feelings about the scene in which Vail confronts her biological mother, Senator Eleanor Linwood, about her past.

5. Is Vail's reaction appropriate and reasonable when she discovers her gun is missing after leaving Deacon's house? What about when Vail goes to Deacon's to pick up Jonathan's book?

6. Did you like Karen Vail as a character, and would you like to read another novel featuring Karen Vail?

7. Why do you think the author chose to make Karen Vail a victim of abuse?

8. What did that tell us about her character in terms of how she deals with other events that happen in the story?

9. Did the killer's diary entries, written in the first person, put you closer to him?

10. The film rights to *The 7th Victim* have been optioned by a major Hollywood producer. What actors/actresses would you cast for the main characters in the movie—Vail; Robby; Bledsoe?

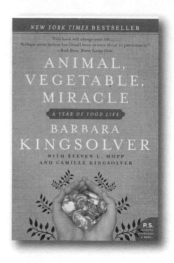

ANIMAL, VEGETABLE, MIRACLE
A Year of Food Life

AUTHORS: *Barbara Kingsolver,*
Steven L. Hopp, **and** *Camille Kingsolver*

PUBLISHER: Harper Perennial, April 2008

WEBSITE: www.kingsolver.com
www.harperperennial.com

AVAILABLE IN:
Trade Paperback, 400 pages, $14.95
ISBN: 978-0-06-085256-6

SUBJECT: Environment/Nature/Culture and
World Issues/Family (Nonfiction)

"Kingsolver takes the genre to a new literary level; a well-paced narrative and the apparent ease of the beautiful prose makes the pages fly. Her tale is both classy and disarming, substantive and entertaining, earnest and funny. . . . More often wry than pious . . . this practical vision of how we might eat . . . is as fresh as just-picked sweet corn."
—Publishers Weekly (starred review)

"With . . . assistance from her husband, Steven, and 19-year-old daughter, Camille, Kingsolver elegantly chronicles a year of back-to-the-land living with her family in Appalachia. . . . Readers frustrated with the unhealthy, artificial food chain will take heart and inspiration here." —Kirkus Reviews

SUMMARY: Author Barbara Kingsolver and her family abandoned the industrial-food pipeline to live a rural life—vowing that, for one year, they'd only buy food raised in their own neighborhood, grow it themselves, or learn to live without it. Part memoir, part journalistic investigation, *Animal, Vegetable, Miracle* is an enthralling narrative that will open your eyes in a hundred new ways to an old truth: You are what you eat.

ABOUT THE AUTHOR: **Barbara Kingsolver's** twelve books of fiction, poetry, and creative nonfiction include the novels *The Bean Trees* and *The Poisonwood Bible*. Translated into nineteen languages, her work has won a devoted worldwide readership and many awards, including the National Humanities Medal. She lives with her family on a farm in southwestern Virginia.

1. What was your perception of America's food industry prior to reading *Animal, Vegetable, Miracle*? What did you learn from this book? How has it altered your views on the way food is acquired and consumed?

2. In what ways, if any, have you changed your eating habits since reading *Animal, Vegetable, Miracle*? Depending on where you live—in an urban, suburban, or rural environment—what other steps would you like to take to modify your lifestyle with regard to eating local?

3. "It had felt arbitrary when we sat around the table with our shopping list, making our rules. It felt almost silly to us in fact, as it may now seem to you. Why impose restrictions on ourselves? Who cares?" asks Kingsolver in *Animal, Vegetable, Miracle*. Did you, in fact, care about Kingsolver's story and find it to be compelling? Why or why not? What was the family's aim for their year-long initiative, and did they accomplish that goal?

4. How does each member of the Kingsolver-Hopp family contribute during their year-long eating adventure? Were you surprised that the author's children not only participated in the endeavor but that they did so with such enthusiasm? Why or why not?

5. How does politics affect America's food production and consumption? What global ramifications are there for the food choices we make?

6. Do you believe that American society can—or will— overcome the need for instant gratification in order to be able to eat seasonally? How does Kingsolver present this aspect in *Animal, Vegetable, Miracle*? Did you get the sense that she and her family ever felt deprived in their eating options?

7. What responsibility do we bear for keeping the environment safe for future generations? How does eating locally factor in to this?

8. Kingsolver asserts that "we have dealt to today's kids the statistical hand of a shorter life expectancy than their parents, which would be us, the ones taking care of them." How is our "thrown-away food culture" a detriment to children's health? She also says, "We're raising our children on the definition of promiscuity if we feed them a casual, indiscriminate mingling of foods from every season plucked from the supermarket." What responsibility do parents have to teach their children about the value and necessity of a local food culture?

9. In what ways do Kingsolver's descriptions of the places she visited on her travels enhance her portrayal of local and seasonal eating?

10. How much of a role do the media play in determining what Americans eat? Discuss the decline of America's diversified family farms, and what it means for the country as a whole.

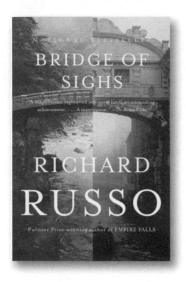

BRIDGE OF SIGHS

AUTHOR: *Richard Russo*

PUBLISHER: Vintage Books, August 2008

WEBSITE: www.ReadingGroupCenter.com

AVAILABLE IN:
Trade Paperback, 656 pages, $14.95
ISBN: 978-1-4000-3090-3

SUBJECT: Family/Relationships/
Identity (Fiction)

"A novel of great warmth, charm and intimacy . . . richly evocative and beautifully wrought." —The New York Times

"A story of constantly evolving complexity and depth. . . . [Bridge of Sighs *is*] *Russo's most intricate, multifaceted novel . . . enormous and enormously moving." —The Washington Post Book World*

"A magnificent, bighearted new novel [*and*] *an astounding achievement. . . . A masterpiece." —The Boston Globe*

"[Russo's] most ambitious and best work." —USA Today

SUMMARY: *Bridge of Sighs*, from the beloved Pulitzer Prize-winning author of *Empire Falls*, is a moving novel about small-town America that expands Russo's widely heralded achievement in ways both familiar and astonishing.

Louis Charles Lynch (also known as Lucy) is sixty years old and has lived in Thomaston, New York, his entire life. He and Sarah, his wife of forty years, are about to embark on a vacation to Italy. Lucy's oldest friend, once a rival for his wife's affection, leads a life in Venice far removed from Thomaston. Perhaps for this reason Lucy is writing the story of his town, his family, and his own life that makes up this rich and mesmerizing novel, interspersed with that of the native son who left so long ago and has never looked back.

ABOUT THE AUTHOR: **Richard Russo** is the author of *Mohawk, The Risk Pool, Straight Man, Nobody's Fool*, and *Empire Falls*, which won the Pulitzer Prize for fiction, and a collection of stories, *The Whore's Child*. He and his wife live in coastal Maine.

1. *Bridge of Sighs* alternates two narratives: Lucy's first-person memoir and the story of Robert Noonan. What are the advantages of this structure? How does it affect the way plot unfolds? Does it influence your impressions of the main characters?

2. How does Lucy's description of Thomaston create an immediate sense of time and place? What details did you find particularly evocative? What does Lucy's tone, as well as the way he presents various facts about Thomaston and its history, reveal about his perceptiveness and his intelligence?

3. Lucy says, "I've always known that there's more going on inside me than finds its way into the world, but this is probably true of everyone. Who doesn't regret that he isn't more fully understood?" To what extent does this feeling lie at the heart of his decision to write his book? Does it play a central role in memoir-writing in general? What else does Lucy hope to accomplish by recalling his past? At the beginning, does he see the dangers, as well as the benefits, of examining his life and the people and events that shaped him?

4. The horrific prank the neighborhood boys play on Lucy triggers the first of many "spells" he will have throughout his life. What is the significance of his spells? What do they reveal about the emotional attachments, anxieties, and doubts that define him both as a child and as an adult?

5. Lucy makes many references to the pursuit of the American Dream and its implications within his own family and in society in general. In what ways did American attitudes in the postwar years embody both the best parts of our national character and its darker undercurrents? What incidents in the novel illuminate the uneasiness and enmity that results from the class, racial, and economic divisions in Thomaston? Do Lucy's beliefs, judgments, and achievements (as a businessman and as a happily married husband and father) color his reconstruction of these events?

6. The Bridge of Sighs in Venice connects the Doge Palace to an adjacent prison, and, as Lucy relates, "Crossing this bridge, the convicts—at least the ones without money or influence—came to understand that all hope was lost." How does the historical function of the bridge, as well as the myths surrounding it, relate to characters' lives? Why has Russo chosen it as the title of the novel?

For the complete Reading Group Guide, visit ReadingGroupCenter.com.

BROKEN COLORS

AUTHOR: *Michele Zackheim*

PUBLISHER: Europa Editions, October 2007

WEBSITE: www.MicheleZackeim.com
www.EuropaEditions.com

AVAILABLE IN:
Trade Paperback, 320 pages, $14.95
ISBN: 978-1-933372-37-2

SUBJECT: Art/Women's Lives/History
(Fiction)

A Book Sense Notable Title

"Zackheim delivers the epic life of a woman whose art and survival become ever more tightly bound with passing years." —Publishers Weekly

"This is a beautiful novel, sometimes comic and always wise." —Library Journal

"I loved Broken Colors *. . . it went into my heart and stayed there."* —Vanessa Redgrave

"With soaring lyricism, Zackheim limns an exquisitely haunting portrait of an indelibly scarred, yet deeply passionate woman." —Booklist

SUMMARY: *Broken Colors* follows the life of painter Sophie Marks. Brushed with moments of passion, heartbreak, and longing, Sophie's journey takes her from World War II England to post-war Paris, to the Italian countryside, to the American Southwest, and back to England where she comes face to face with hidden memories.

ABOUT THE AUTHOR: **Michele Zackheim** was a visual artist before turning to writing. Her work has been exhibited in galleries and museums in the United States and Europe. She is the author of *Violette's Embrace* and *Einstein's Daughter: The Search for Lieserl*. She lives in New York City with her husband, the sculptor Charles Ramsburg.

1. *Broken Colors* is a novel punctuated by a speckling of quotes from famous authors and writers. Do the quotes help develop the theme of the novel?

2. What is the correlation between travel and age in this novel? Does Sophie's constant relocating match her shifting emotional landscape, and are the two inextricably tied? Is Sophie in Paris different then Sophie in the American Southwest?

3. If Sophie's grandfather hadn't taught her to paint, would she have turned to art as a necessary form of expression?

4. Early in the novel, Sophie meets a fellow painter, Major Roderick, whose face is grotesquely disfigured with partial vision. What is the significance of this character at that point in Sophie's journey?

5. What was your reaction when Sophie first met Luca? Is it important that they're both artists?

6. How do you feel about setting art against the backdrop of war and loss? Does it make art feel like a more vital human resource?

7. On page 230, Sophie explains what the term 'broken colors' means? Do you think the book is aptly titled? Is this a strong metaphor for Sophie's life?

8. As a reader, were you rooting for the character of Luca to return to Sophie's life? Were you surprised by his re-introduction in the latter part of the novel?

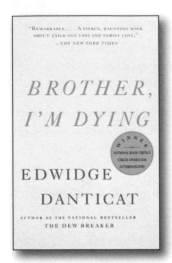

BROTHER, I'M DYING

AUTHOR: *Edwidge Danticat*

PUBLISHER: Vintage Books, September 2008

WEBSITE: www.ReadingGroupCenter.com

AVAILABLE IN:
Trade Paperback, 288 pages, $14.95
ISBN: 978-1-4000-3430-7

SUBJECT: Family/Culture & World Issues/
Identity (Memoir)

"[Danticat] has written a fierce, haunting book about exile and loss and family love, and how that love can survive distance and separation, loss and abandonment and somehow endure, undented and robust. . . . Moving." —**Michiko Kakutani, *The New York Times***

SUMMARY: From the best-selling author of *The Dew Breaker*, a major work of nonfiction: a powerfully moving family story that centers around the men closest to her heart—her father, Mira, and his older brother, Joseph.

But *Brother, I'm Dying* soon becomes a terrifying tale of good people caught up in events beyond their control. Late in 2004, his life threatened by an angry mob, forced to flee his church, the frail, eighty-one-year-old Joseph makes his way to Miami from his home in Haiti, where he thinks he will be safe. Instead, he is detained by U.S. Customs, held by the Department of Homeland Security, brutally imprisoned, and dead within days. It was a story that made headlines around the world. His brother, Mira, will soon join him in death, but not before he holds hope in his arms: Edwidge's firstborn, who will bear his name—and the family's stories, both joyous and tragic—into the next generation.

ABOUT THE AUTHOR: **Edwidge Danticat** is the author of numerous books, including *Breath, Eyes, Memory; Krik? Krak!*, a National Book Award finalist; *The Farming of Bones*, an American Book Award winner; and *The Dew Breaker,* a PEN/Faulkner Award finalist and winner of the first Story Prize. She lives in Miami with her husband and daughter.

1. Danticat tells us that she has constructed the story from the "borrowed recollections of family members. . . . What I learned from my father and uncle, I learned out of sequence and in fragments. This is an attempt at cohesiveness, and at re-creating a few wondrous and terrible months when their lives and mine intersected in startling ways, forcing me to look forward and back at the same time". Discuss what this work of reconstruction and reordering means for the structure of the story she presents, as well as for her own understanding of what happened to the two brothers.

2. How does young Edwidge retain her loyalties to her parents, even though they are absent from her life for so many years? Is there evidence that she feels hurt or rejected by their decision to leave for the States? How does she feel when they come back to visit Haiti with two new children?

3. While many readers will know that Haiti was a slave colony, why is the fact of the American invasion and nineteen-year occupation less well known? Danticat's paternal grandfather, Granpè Nozial, fought with the guerrilla resistance against the Americans. How does the family's engagement with Haiti's political history affect Joseph's unwillingness to emigrate to the U.S.? Why does he refuse to leave Haiti, or even to remove himself from the dangers of Bel Air?

4. Danticat says of her story, "I am writing this only because they can't". As a girl, Edwidge was often literally her uncle's voice, because after his tracheotomy she could read his lips and tell others what he was saying. Why is it important that she also speak for her father and her uncle in writing this memoir?

5. Consider the relationship between the two brothers, Mira and Joseph. There is a significant difference in age, and Mira has been away from his brother for decades, by the end of the story. Despite this, they remain close. What assumptions about kinship and family ties are displayed in their love for each other? Are these bonds similar to, or stronger than, ties you would see between American-born brothers?

6. How does Danticat convey a sense of the richness of Haitian culture? What are the people like? What are their folk tales like? How does their use of both Creole and French affect their approach to language and speech? How does she make us feel the effects of the violence and poverty that the Haitians endure?

For the complete Reading Group Guide, visit ReadingGroupCenter.com.

CHARITY GIRL

AUTHOR: *Michael Lowenthal*

PUBLISHER: Mariner Books, January 2008

WEBSITE: www.marinerbooks.com
www.MichaelLowenthal.com

AVAILABLE IN:
Trade Paperback, 336 pages, $13.95
ISBN: 978-0-618-91978-9

SUBJECT: Women's Lives/
American History/Identity (Fiction)

"Lively and illuminating . . . marr[ies] the facts of history with the details that make a fictional life come alive." —*Washington Post Book World,* **Anita Shreve, author of** *Testimony*

"Even while capturing the great sweep of the period, Charity Girl *celebrates most the depth of the characters' lives."* —**Matthew Pearl, author of** *The Poe Shadow*

SUMMARY: During World War I, seventeen-year-old Frieda Mintz secures a job at a Boston department store and strikes out on her own, escaping her repressive Jewish mother and marriage to a wealthy widower twice her age. She is intoxicated by her newfound freedom and the patriotic fervor of the day. That is, until a soldier reports her as his last sexual contact, sweeping her up in the government's wartime crusade against venereal disease. Quarantined in a detention center, Frieda finds in the Home's confines a group of brash, unforgettable women who help her see the way to a new kind of independence. *Charity Girl* is based on a little-known chapter in American history that saw fifteen thousand women across the nation incarcerated. Lowenthal's poignant, provocative novel will leave readers moved—and astonished by the shameful facts that inspired it.

ABOUT THE AUTHOR: **Michael Lowenthal** grew up near Washington, D.C., and graduated from Dartmouth College. He is the author of two previous novels, *Avoidance* and *The Same Embrace,* as well as short stories and essays that have been widely anthologized. Lowenthal teaches creative writing in the MFA program at Lesley University. He also serves on the executive board of PEN New England.

1. At the center of the novel hangs an ethical dilemma, wherein the rights of the few are weighed against the health and safety of many. Would you consider the government's moral crusade reasonable, given the circumstances of wartime? In what other way might the need to maintain a healthy army have been addressed? In what circumstances do we face similar choices today?

2. Does Frieda seem particularly rebellious or attracted to danger, or is she more a regular girl trapped in a series of bad situations? Placed in her situation, would you have made the same choices that she did? How does Frieda change during the course of the book?

3. *Charity Girl* opens in Boston in 1918; at the time, employment choices for women were limited. Why does the prospect of being a shopgirl at Jordan Marsh so appeal to Frieda? Aside from her wages, how does her job benefit her?

4. Frieda moves to a boarding house in the city as a form of self-imposed exile from her mother and their Russian immigrant community. What other instances of banishment and displacement are found in the novel? How do these instances resonate with each other?

5. Do you agree with Mrs. Sprague's assessment that the so-called "charity girls" are more a threat than prostitutes? Were these "charity girls" exploited, do you think, by their employers, by their suitors?

6. Did you find Felix an honorable character? What clues does Lowenthal give about his true regard for Frieda? Why does Frieda hold such unwavering belief in the rightness of his actions?

7. What factors contributed to these women's diverse reactions to their fate? How do you think you might have responded if you had found yourself indefinitely detained?

8. What motivates Mrs. Sprague or Alice Longley or Dr. Slocum to be party to the government's detention program? Is their participation defensible?

9. The novel's epigram reads: "Charity causes half the suffering she relieves, but she cannot relieve half the suffering she has caused." What do you think this means in the context of the novel? If charity comes with real or perceived strings attached, can it be true charity?

10. How is the experience of reading Frieda's story different from reading nonfiction accounts of the time? How, if at all, does the novelist's modern perspective color the way he portrays historical characters and events? What draws you to historical novels?

11. Do you think, in the end, that Frieda finds redemption? What do you imagine her life is like after the War? What does the final sequence tell you about her fate? Is it an ending you would have wished for her?

CHEZ MOI

AUTHOR: *Agnès Desarthe*
Adriana Hunter, Translator

PUBLISHER: Penguin Books, April 2008

WEBSITE: www.penguin.com

AVAILABLE IN:
Trade Paperback, 272 pages, $14.00
ISBN: 978-0-143-11323-2

SUBJECT: Relationships/Women's Lives/
Family (Fiction)

"This lovely book is a cassoulet bulging with lush, delectable descriptions of cuisine and straight-shooting observations on life. Myriam's restaurant has as much to do with improvising ways of living, loving and finding one's way home again as with eating well. It's a frothy, complex pleasure to linger there with her." —**Publisher Weekly**

SUMMARY: At forty-three, Myriam has been a wife, mother, and lover—but never a restauranteur. When she opens Chez Moi in a quiet neighborhood in Paris, she has no idea how to run a business, but armed only with her love of cooking, she is determined to try. But soon enough her delectable cuisine brings her many neighbors to Chez Moi, and Myriam finds that she may get a second chance at life and love. *Chez Moi* is a charming story that will appeal to the many readers who fell in love with Joanne Harris's *Chocolat* and Laura Esquivel's *Like Water for Chocolate*.

ABOUT THE AUTHOR: **Agnès Desarthe** was born in Paris in 1966. She has had two previous novels translated into English: *Five Photos of My Wife* (2001), which was short-listed for both the Independent Foreign Fiction Prize and the Jewish Quarterly Fiction Prize, and *Good Intentions* (2002). *Chez Moi* is her first book to be published in the U.S. **Adriana Hunter** has been working as a literary translator since 1998 and has now translated more than thirty books from the French, including two other novels by Agnès Desarthe.

1. Myriam says she cooks "with and out of love, yet is unable to feel love for her son. Is it possible to stop loving your child? What circumstances do you believe would cause something like that to happen?

2. The way Myriam describes flowers and food is deeply affectionate and almost anthropomorphic. Why do you think she is able to so lushly convey her love for these things, yet have such trouble with people?

3. Where you surprised by Rainer's slap and the aftermath? Do you believe that love can die so suddenly? What are some other reasons that could cause a relationship to end swiftly and without argument?

4. When Myriam's betrayal and the reason for her abandonment are revealed, does it change your view of her? How were you able to understand or empathize with her unfaithfulness? If you were in her position, would you have made the same decision to leave?

5. Myriam has elaborate, realistic dreams that reflect her state of mind and desires. Why do you think she remembers them so clearly? What affect do they have on her? How do your own dreams affect your waking life?

6. At the end of *Chez Moi*, Hugo and Myriam reunite after six years apart. It can be argued that often it is much easier to remain estranged from a person than to make strides to patch things up. Have you had an experience in your own life when you had to choose whether or not to repair a relationship that had grown distant? Who made the first move towards contact, and how did it work out in the end? Was it worth the effort?

7. Ali tells Myriam, "You're the wildest person I've ever met." Myriam has taken such risks in her life but in her mind, she is merely a cook. Why do you think she's still so unaware of others' perceptions of her? Do you think your own self-perception is accurate? Are you surprised at what others see in you?

8. Myriam feels that she needs to leave behind the restaurant and everything that she's created if she's going to give herself wholly to Ali. What did the restaurant say about her that has now changed? Do you agree with her decision?

9. Desire, physical and emotional, plays a large role in the book. So does destiny. How are the ideas of desire and destiny intertwined? Do you think it is possible to will something to happen?

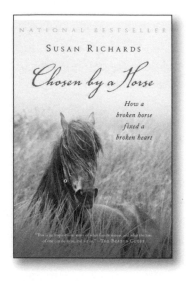

CHOSEN BY A HORSE
How a Broken Horse
Fixed a Broken Heart

AUTHOR: *Susan Richards*

PUBLISHER: Mariner Books, June 2007

WEBSITE: www.susan-richards.com
www.marinerbooks.com

AVAILABLE IN:
Trade Paperback, 258 pages, $13.00
ISBN: 978-0-156-03117-2

SUBJECT: Family/Personal Discovery/
Nature (Memoir)

*"This is an inspirational story of what family means, and what the loss of one can do to us, and for us." —***The Boston Globe**

*"Two kindred spirits find each other in this beautifully written memoir about the human-animal bond." —***Temple Grandin, author of** *Animals in Translation*

"Susan Richards thought she was rescuing a starved, abused and abandoned mare. Turns out Lay Me Down was rescuing Susan Richards. An incredibly moving story, beautifully written and insightful."
*—***The Roanoke Times**

*"Important lessons about courage, kindness and grief." —***The Hartford Courant**

SUMMARY: The horse Susan Richards chose for rescue wouldn't be corralled into her waiting trailer. But Lay Me Down, a former racehorse with a foal close on her heels, walked right up that ramp and into Susan's life. Weak from malnutrition, Lay Me Down had endured a rough road, but somehow her heart was still open and generous. Then fate brought her into Susan's paddock, where she taught this brokenhearted women how to embrace the joys of life despite the dangers of living.

ABOUT THE AUTHOR: **Susan Richards** has a BA in English from the University of Colorado and a Master of Social Work degree from Adelphi University. She lives in Bearsville, New York, and teaches writing at SUNY Ulster and Marist College.

1. How are Susan's horses a substitute for a human family? What needs do they fulfill that people in her life cannot? Does Susan use her horses to escape from "real life" (the pressures of romantic relationships, loneliness, et cetera), or do they represent it?

2. How do Susan's past struggles—the loss of her parents, her abusive childhood, her alcoholism, and her divorce—continue to affect her life on a daily basis so many decades later?

3. Did this book remind you of any of your childhood favorites? In what ways?

4. What about Georgia's personality makes her lovable as a horse but not as a person?

5. What function does Hank serve in Susan's life? Would she have been better off if he had not called her six years later? If he had not been allergic to horses, would Susan have been able to commit herself to him as a partner?

6. How do Susan's feelings about her horse's name change as her memoir progresses? How do you feel about Lay Me Down's name by the close of the book?

7. What does Lay Me Down's calm and trusting demeanor, even after a traumatic past, say about the "nature versus nurture" argument?

8. In what way do you feel the author was "chosen" by Lay Me Down? Could she have been chosen by another person, or another animal, and still have learned the same lessons about her life that she learns in this book?

9. Animals are often said to possess healing influences—some studies suggest that elderly people who keep pets have lower rates of heart disease, stroke, and depression. What do you think it is about animals that humans find so calming? Is this something humans can't provide for each other? Do you have a particular pet that seemed to have a special effect on you?

10. In caring for Lay Me Down Susan is forced to confront illness head on. How does this help Susan grow, heal, and come to terms with her past?

11. How does Lay Me Down's death affect Susan? Is this a normal reaction to the loss of an animal friend? If not, how and why?

12. What do you think the author has learned through the events described in the book? Would Susan's life have been easier, and less painful, if she had avoided an emotional connection with a damaged horse? Can we arrange our lives in ways that help us to avoid suffering? If so, at what cost?

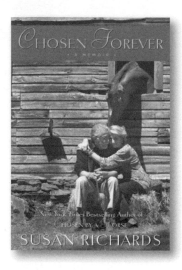

CHOSEN FOREVER

AUTHOR: *Susan Richards*

PUBLISHER: Soho Press, June 2008

WEBSITE: www.sohopress.com
www.susanrichards.com

AVAILABLE IN:
Hardcover, 288 pages, $23.00
ISBN: 978-1-56947-492-1

SUBJECT: Women's Lives/Identity/
Relationships (Memoir)

"Richards reflects on how rich life becomes when one travels her own best path. . . . Richards writes more courageously than she perhaps realizes, and each page of this uplifting book will touch a chord in everyone who enjoyed her first book." —Booklist

"Charismatic. . . Engaging writing by an honest self-explorer." —Kirkus Reviews

SUMMARY: When Susan Richards adopted an abused horse rescued by the local SPCA she didn't know how Lay Me Down's loving nature would touch her heart—and change her life.

Susan, a writing teacher, had lost her mother at the age of five and been abandoned by her father to uncaring relatives; she had an unhappy marriage ending in divorce and had self-medicated for anxiety (and grief and repressed anger) with alcohol. For more than a decade she had aspired to be a published writer but it was only with the memoir she wrote to honor Lay Me Down that she achieved this goal.

The book led to a book tour, in the course of which Susan reconnected with family and friends with whom she had severed relations. But even more joyously, at the second reading on her tour she met the man who had sold her his house twenty-four years earlier, a world famous photographer, Dennis Stock. And they fell in love.

ABOUT THE AUTHOR: **Susan Richards** lives in Bearsville, New York, with her husband Dennis Stock and their four dogs and one cat.

1. Is perseverance as important as inspiration to a would-be writer?

2. Can a woman inspire love if she thinks she's unattractive?

3. Do you think that the more than twenty-year age difference between Susan and Dennis should have prevented them from marrying?

4. How do animals differ from humans as catalysts for change?

5. The advantages of wealth are myriad. What are the disadvantages?

6. What makes "home" different from anywhere else?

7. What are the challenges older couples face when trying to integrate their lives?

8. Has a seemingly random "sign" ever helped you make a decision?

9. What accounts for the current popularity of memoirs? What do people want from a memoir?

10. Did you learn things about the inside of the publishing world that surprised you? Did you think that publishers and writers all made a lot of money right away?

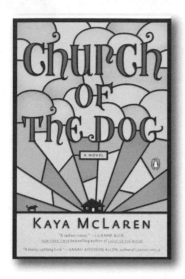

CHURCH OF THE DOG

AUTHOR: *Kaya McLaren*

PUBLISHER: Penguin Books, May 2008

WEBSITE: www.penguin.com
www.kayamclaren.com

AVAILABLE IN:
Trade Paperback, 240 pages, $13.00
ISBN: 978-0-143-11342-3

SUBJECT: Relationships/Inspiration/
Family (Fiction)

"With prose as clear and pure as mountain water, Kaya McLaren has written a testament to the plain sense of things. Church of the Dog *is spiritual, even a little magical, but it's also incredibly practical. McLaren has a glorious way of finding beauty in the bigger picture. A lovely, uplifting book."*
—**Sarah Addison Allen, author of** *Garden Spells* **and** *The Sugar Queen*

"What a genuinely surprising novel Kaya McLaren has written, with characters that are each, in their own way, quietly magical and also heartbreakingly true. Like Barbara Kingsolver's early heroines, Mara O'Shaunessey lives in the real world but reminds us, in all her actions, that animals can be messengers of truth and love has transformative powers." —**Cammie McGovern, author of** *Eye Contact*

SUMMARY: Deep in Oregon farm country, Edith and Earl McRae are looking down the barrel of their fiftieth anniversary with none of the joy such a milestone should hold. Instead, they are stuck in a past that holds them to heartbreak and tragedy. Enter the magical Mara O'Shaunessey who appears on their ranch with the power to mend long broken fences and show them how to recognize the enchantment of their everyday lives. Kaya McLaren's story of redemption and rediscovery will inspire readers to find the magic and power in every day shared with the people they love.

ABOUT THE AUTHOR: **Kaya McLaren** teaches art and lives on the east slope of Snoqualmie Pass in Washington state with her dog, Big Cedar. Her second novel, *On the Divinity of Second Chances*, will be published by Penguin in winter 2009.

1. If you could travel in your sleep, where would you go? What companions would you like to accompany you?

2. Daniel wonders if "the only way to freedom is through devastation." What are some other instances where renewal comes from destruction? Are there are other ways to reach freedom and renewal? What are they?

3. Mara isn't sure she has had an impact on her students. What are your vivid memories of teachers that influenced your own life?

4. Daniel is angry that the funerals of his mother and father, and later, his grandfather, seem insulting to the very people they are meant to honor. Who are funerals really for, the living or the dead? Should clergy respect the varied religious traditions that might be represented or tailor services to fit only the religion of the deceased?

5. Edith can't seem to give Earl's clothes and effects away and her son's room is still as he left it. She reflects that her mother got rid of all Edith's father's personal items almost immediately after his death. Which way of coping with a death do you think is healthier? Why?

6. Mara questions Daniel about his negatives—photographic negatives, that is. What are some projects you have not seen through? Why did you abandon them?

7. Kelli attempts to abandon her newborn with Mara and Daniel. How would you react if someone tried to leave a baby with you? Could you open your home to someone in Kelli's situation, despite the possibility of its affecting your own life in a significant way?

8. In her dreams, Mara has traveled near the edge of Heaven several times. Is Mara truly in Heaven, or is it just a construct of her own imagination? What do you picture when you think of Heaven?

9. Mara collects quite a few pets through the course of the novel, beginning with Harvey, her pig. What personality traits do you look for in a dog or other sort of pet? In a friend? In what ways do they overlap? Would you consider one of your pets to be a guardian angel?

10. The author chose to use four different narrators in *Church of the Dog*, Mara, Earl, Edith, and Daniel. Did you find that you missed any of the characters after they stopped telling the story from their points of view?

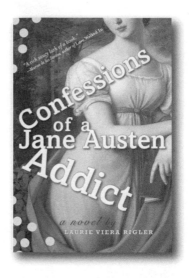

CONFESSIONS OF A JANE AUSTEN ADDICT

AUTHOR: *Laurie Rigler*

PUBLISHER: Plume Books, May 2008

WEBSITE: www.plumebooks.com
www.janeaustenaddict.com

AVAILABLE IN:
Trade Paperback, 304 pages, $14.00
ISBN: 978-0-452-28972-7

SUBJECT: Humor/Relationships/Identity
(Fiction)

"A rich, saucy lark of a book for all of us who have ever looked at our lives and marveled, 'How did I get here?'" —**Marisa de los Santos, author of** *Love Walked In*

"You don't have to be a rabid fan of Jane Austen to enjoy Laurie Viera Rigler's entertainingly funny love story. A fun read." —*Social Life Magazine*

SUMMARY: After nursing a broken engagement with Jane Austen novels and Absolut, Courtney Stone wakes up and finds herself not in her Los Angeles bedroom or even in her own body, but inside the bedchamber of a woman in Regency England. Who but an Austen addict like herself could concoct such a fantasy? Try as she might to control her mind and find a way home, Courtney cannot deny that she is becoming this other woman—and being this other woman is not without its advantages.

ABOUT THE AUTHOR: **Laurie Rigler** is a freelance book editor who teaches writing workshops, including classes at Vroman's, Southern California's oldest and largest independent bookstore. She graduated summa cum laude, Phi Beta Kappa, from the State University of New York at Buffalo with a B.A. in Classics.

1. Would you have handled things differently if you found yourself in Courtney's/Jane's situation? Which things would you have done differently? Which things would you have done the same?

2. How does Courtney/Jane use Jane Austen's novels as a means of making sense of her world? Have you ever turned to your favorite books or films for inner strength, guidance, or comfort?

3. How do you interpret the ending of the book?

4. Aside from the societal restrictions on a woman's mobility, career choices, and living arrangements that Courtney/Jane faced in 1813, have parental, peer, and personal attitudes toward unmarried women fundamentally changed since Jane Austen's day?

5. One of the ways in which Courtney/Jane defines herself is by what she reads. To what extent do we define ourselves by what we read? To what extent do we form our opinions of others based on what they read?

6. Like Courtney/Jane, have you ever found yourself in a situation where your very concept of who you are was fundamentally challenged?

7. What are the things you think you would enjoy the most about being in Jane Austen's world? What are the things you might find particularly challenging? Is there anything in the contemporary world that you absolutely could not do without?

8. If it were possible for you to be someone in Jane Austen's world, who would you wish to be? Would you prefer a round-trip ticket to that world, or one-way only?

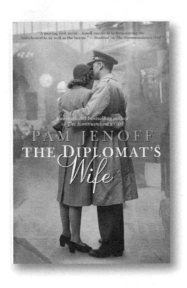

THE DIPLOMAT'S WIFE

AUTHOR: *Pam Jenoff*

PUBLISHER: Harlequin Enterprises Ltd, May 2008

WEBSITE: www.eHarlequin.com
www.eBooks.eHarlequin.com

AVAILABLE IN:
Trade Paperback, 360 pages, $13.95
ISBN: 978-0-7783-2512-3

ALSO AVAILABLE IN:
eBook, 360 pages, $12.55
ISBN: 978-1-4268-1612-3

SUBJECT: Relationships/Personal Challenges/
Cultural & World Issues (Historical Fiction)

"Jenoff's stirring sequel to her debut, The Kommandant's Girl. . . . *Historical romance fans will be well rewarded"* —**Publishers Weekly (starred review)**

SUMMARY: How have I been lucky enough to come here, to be alive, when so many others are not? I should have died. . . . But I am here.

1945. Surviving the brutality of a Nazi prison camp, Marta Nederman is lucky to have escaped with her life. Recovering from the horror, she meets Paul, an American soldier who gives her hope of a happier future. But their plans to meet in London are dashed when Paul's plane crashes.

Devastated and pregnant, Marta marries Simon, a caring British diplomat, and glimpses the joy that home and family can bring. But her happiness is threatened when she learns of a Communist spy in British intelligence, and that the one person who can expose the traitor is connected to her past.

ABOUT THE AUTHOR: **Pam Jenoff** was born in Maryland and raised in southern New Jersey. A bachelor's degree magna cum laude in international affairs, led her to work as a foreign service officer with the State Department assigned to the U.S. consulate in Kraków, Poland. Here, Pam developed her expertise in Polish-Jewish relations and the Holocaust by working on matters such as preservation of Auschwitz and the restitution of Jewish property in Poland. In 1998, she attended law school at the University of Pennsylvania and now lives in Philadelphia where she works as an attorney. *The Diplomat's Wife* is the follow-up to her first novel, *The Kommandant's Girl*, which was nominated for a Quill Award.

1. How do you think Marta's experiences during the war have affected her?

2. What do you think draws Marta and Paul together so powerfully?

3. How did Marta's character change/evolve throughout the story?

4. What was Marta's greatest strength? Her greatest flaw?

5. How does Marta and Paul's dynamic change through the book?

6. What was Marta's relationship like with the places and people from her past?

7. Did you agree with Marta's choices in the book? Why or why not?

8. How was Marta's life affected by the secrets that she kept?

9. How did Marta and Emma's views of one another change in this book?

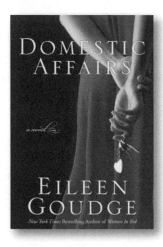

DOMESTIC AFFAIRS

AUTHOR: *Eileen Goudge*

PUBLISHER: Vanguard Press, June 2008

WEBSITE: www.domesticaffairsbook.com
www.eileengoudge.com

AVAILABLE IN:
Hardcover, 448 pages, $25.95
ISBN: 978-1-593-15475-2

SUBJECT: Relationships/Family/
Women's Lives (Fiction)

"Eileen Goudge deftly weaves multiple storylines into a seamless page-turner propelled by juicy secrets, skeletons in the closet, stunning betrayals and heart-wrenching reunions. If you're feeling nostalgic for a good, old-fashioned sprawling saga, Domestic Affairs *is your book."* —**Wendy Corsi Staub,** *New York Times* **bestselling author of** *Dying Breath*

"Eileen Goudge, author of Woman in Red, *has written a beautiful and heart-wrenching story of the love and closeness two women share as teens only to be destroyed. Now they share a need to take solace in each other and restore their once-close relationship. This story will reach into your soul and place you into the characters' thoughts. Highly recommended reading!"—FreshFiction*

SUMMARY: From the *New York Times* bestselling author of *Woman in Red* comes an intimate story of friendship lost and regained, old loves rekindled, and a baptism by fire that ultimately leads to the redemption of three very special women. In this sweeping emotional tale, Abigail, Lila, and Concepción are thrown together and forced to unite in order to save one another . . . and themselves. Along the way they discover that the forces that have torn their lives apart have also shaped them in ways they never could have imagined.

ABOUT THE AUTHOR: **Eileen Goudge** is the *New York Times* best-selling author whose novels include *One Last Dance, Garden of Lies, Thorns of Truth,* and *Woman in Red* . There are more than three million copies of her books in print worldwide. She lives in New York City with her husband, entertainment reporter Sandy Kenyon.

1. Friendships are the foundations of our lives. Have you ever been betrayed by a best friend? If so, how has it affected you? Did the friendship survive?

2. Abigail is like many women, in the sense that she feels she has to do it all. How do you juggle work and family? What are the challenges and how have you met them?

3. *Domestic Affairs* is about the power of secrets to affect our lives. Have you ever harbored a secret that changed the course of your life? How might it have been different had you revealed the secret?

4. Lila loses everything in one fell swoop: her husband, home, and the security she's known. Have you ever been "down and out"? If so, how did you handle it?

5. The grieving Mexican mother, Concepción, crosses the border into this country illegally. Did you come away with a deeper understanding of this social issue in reading the book? What are your feelings about illegal immigrants in this country?

6. The two teenagers in the book enter into an unthinkable pact. Where do you draw the line with teenage children? How much privacy should they be allowed and when is it time to step in when you suspect they're hiding something?

7. Abigail and Vaughn reconnect after a period of many years and the spark they generated as teenagers is reignited. Do you ever wonder what would happen if an old love reentered your life? Has that ever happened?

8. Lila rejects the advances of her suitor Karim at first. After losing her husband, she's not sure she can take the risk of having something like that happen to her again. What would make you fall in love again after such a tragic loss? What would a man (or woman) have to do to prove worthy of taking that risk?

9. Ultimately, *Domestic Affairs* is about redemption. In this case, two women find redemption after initially seeking revenge. Do you know anyone for whom this has been the case? Would you be able to forgive someone who betrayed you or cost you the life of a loved one?

DRIVING WITH DEAD PEOPLE

AUTHOR: *Monica Holloway*

PUBLISHER: Simon Spotlight Entertainment
March 2008

WEBSITE: www.simonsays.com

AVAILABLE IN:
Trade Paperback, 336 pages, $14.00
ISBN: 978-1-4169-5512-2

SUBJECT: Family/Relationships/Identity
(Memoir)

"Memoir, at its best, opens my heart and gives me a view into the core perfection of another. Monica does this in the most essential way, going directly to perfect storytelling laced with irony and humor. She held my heart with her raw, unapologetic honesty, and she flawlessly rendered what it is like to be a child who sees everything, endures it, and still loves with her whole being." — **Jennifer Lauck, *New York Times* bestselling author of *Blackbird and Still Waters***

"A meticulously reported account of one girl's journey through a violent and unpredictable childhood. Holloway's strong voice and remarkable sense of humor, in spite of the horror in her past, make this an unforgettable read." —**Hope Edelman, *New York Times* bestselling author of *Motherless Daughters***

SUMMARY: Small wonder that, at nine-years-old, Monica Holloway develops a fascination with the local funeral home. With a father who drives his Ford pickup with a Kodak movie camera sitting shotgun just in case he sees an accident, and whose home movies feature more footage of disasters than of his children, Monica is primed to become a morbid child.

Throughout this remarkable memoir of her dysfunctional, eccentric, and wholly unforgettable family, Monica Holloway's prose shines with humor, clear-eyed grace, and an uncommon sense of resilience.

ABOUT THE AUTHOR: **Monica Holloway** is an actress turned writer whose essay "Red Boots and Cole Haans" was described by *Newsday* as "brilliant, grimly hilarious." This is her first full-length book.

1. The first story Monica tells is of reading about Sarah Keeler's death and attending her funeral. Why do you think, as she says in the first sentence, that this "changes everything"? How does it set the stage for the rest of the memoir?

2. Monica describes her mother as "a human cork; she floated to the top of any awful situation." What are some examples that support her description? Are there any instances when her mother behaves differently? Did your opinion of her mother change at all over the course of the book?

3. Monica is in an almost constant state of anxiety. What are the physical effects of her fear and uncertainty? What effects are less obvious?

4. What does Monica learn about herself when confronted with the possibility of death? Why does she like to imagine being dead?

5. The Kilner household (and funeral home) becomes a haven for Monica—a home away from home. What does their family—especially Julie and Dave—offer her? How do they influence her?

6. Describe the relationship Monica has with each of her sisters. How does each relationship evolve? Why do Becky and Monica grow apart in high school, at a time when they need each other most? How does JoAnn take over that role in Monica's life?

7. What attracts Monica to acting? How do you think her childhood experience might help to make her an especially gifted performer?

8. How does Monica's mother act after the divorce? How does her father?

9. Discuss Monica's relationships with men. Do you think it would ever have been possible for her to have a fulfilling relationship with a man before she remembered and dealt with her sexual abuse?

10. How does their childhood trauma shape each of the Peterson's adult lives and choices? Did their ways of coping as adults change or remain the same from when they were young?

11. Were you surprised when, as an adult, Monica grew close to her father? Why do you think this occurred when it did?

12. Do you think that Monica's mother was aware of the abuse?

13. What character traits—both good and bad—do you think Monica developed as a result of her early years and how did those traits shape her life?

14. How might the memories of other members of her family differ from Monica's own? Discuss how she handles writing from JoAnn's perspective in part five of the book.

15. Which parts of the book were the most difficult to read and which did you enjoy the most? Discuss her writing style and how she confronts the most sensitive and personal parts of her past.

ESCAPE

AUTHOR: *Carolyn Jessop*
with *Laura Palmer*

PUBLISHER: Broadway Books, January 2009

WEBSITE: www.broadwaybooks.com

AVAILABLE IN:
Trade Paperback, 432 pages, $14.95
ISBN: 978-0-7679-2757-4

SUBJECT: Family/Women's Lives/Faith
(Memoir)

"Jessop's courageous, heart-wrenching account is absolutely factual. This riveting book reminds us that truth can indeed be much, much stranger than fiction." —**Jon Krakauer, author of** *Under the Banner of Heaven, Into Thin Air,* **and** *Into the Wild*

SUMMARY: A *New York Times* bestseller with more than 100,000 copies sold in hardcover, *Escape* is the dramatic account of life inside an ultra-fundamentalist sect, and one woman's courageous flight to freedom with her children.

When she was eighteen years old, Carolyn Jessop was coerced into an arranged marriage with Merril Jessop, a man thirty-two years her senior who already had three wives. She was born into and raised in the Fundamentalist Church of Jesus Christ of Latter-day Saints (FLDS). Over time, Jessop had eight children and withstood her husband's psychological abuse. No woman in the country had ever escaped from the FLDS and managed to get her children out, too. In 2003, Jessop chose freedom over fear and fled—with her children. She had twenty dollars to her name.

ABOUT THE AUTHOR: **Carolyn Jessop** was born into the Fundamentalist Church of Jesus Christ of Latter-Day Saints and spent most of her life in Colorado City, Arizona. Since leaving the group in 2003, she has lived in West Jordon, Utah, with her eight children. **Laura Palmer** is the author of *Shrapnel in the Heart* and collaborated on five other books, the most recent being *To Catch a Predator* with NBC's Chris Hansen. She lives in New York City.

1. How did Carolyn's spirit of survival help her throughout her life? What gave her the courage to ultimately escape her fate?

2. How is religion used to justify FLDS beliefs about sex, marriage, and parenting? How do these beliefs affect the daily lives of FLDS members? How are women particularly affected by the risk of sexual shame?

3. What are the biggest differences in the way men and women are treated in the FLDS? How does this influence the relationships between spouses?

4. Discuss the dynamics between the wives described by Carolyn. How did the situation cause cruel behavior, often driven by scarce resources?

5. Why do you think polygamy has continued to exist in the modern world? Are there any advantages to living in such a situation?

6. How do Carolyn's recollections of her childhood both sustain her and haunt her? What did her two mothers teach her about the role of women in the world?

7. How would you describe the FLDS's attitude toward healthcare?

8. How do FLDS children adapt to living in extremely large families? How are favoritism and competition handled? How does this experience shape the way they view the world and their relationships with others?

9. What are your thoughts about decriminalizing polygamy ? How far do you believe legislators can go in dictating behaviors that contradict religious beliefs?

10. How did you react when Carolyn described the ex-convict who began working at her husband's motel? Why didn't Merril care about her personal safety? How was Colorado City affected by the fact that the FLDS controlled local law enforcement?

11. After 9/11, what led so many people in the FLDS to follow Jeffs's apocalyptic preaching at that point?

12. How was money managed in Carolyn's family and within the FLDS? How did Carolyn learn to make do and become a good provider for her family?

13. How have the FLDS and other cults survived in America, despite widespread media attention? Will this ever change? What are your reasons for this prediction?

14. Education is tightly controlled by the FLDS. What led Carolyn to graduate from college, despite constant obstacles?

15. How has her story affected the way you see your own life? What actions are you inspired to take to help other victimized women and children in your community, or elsewhere in the world?

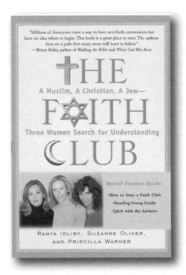

THE FAITH CLUB
A Muslim, A Christian, A Jew—
Three Women Search for Understanding

AUTHORS: **Ranya Idliby, Suzanne Oliver,** and **Priscilla Warner**

PUBLISHER: Free Press, June 2007

WEBSITE: www.thefaithclub.com
www.simonsays.com

AVAILABLE IN:
Trade Paperback, 416 pages, $14.00
ISBN: 978-0-7432-9048-7

SUBJECT: Faith/Women's Lives/
Personal Challenges (Nonfiction)

"More Fight Club than book club, the coauthors pull no punches; their outstanding honesty makes for a page-turning read, rare for a religion nonfiction book . . . almost every taboo topic is explored on this engaging spiritual ride." —**Publishers Weekly**

"Millions of Americans crave a way to have interfaith conversation but have no idea where to begin. This book is a great place to start. The authors have set a path that many more will want to follow." —**Bruce Feiler, author of** *Walking the Bible* **and** *Where God Was Born*

SUMMARY: The Faith Club was started when Ranya Idliby, an American Muslim of Palestinian descent, recruited Suzanne Oliver, a Christian, and Priscilla Warner, a Jew, to write about their three religions. With courage, pain, and sometimes tears, these women found themselves completely transformed by their experience inside the safe cocoon of the Faith Club. This is their story.

ABOUT THE AUTHORS: **Ranya Idliby** graduated from Georgetown University's School of Foreign Service and earned her MS in international relations from the London School of Economics. She lives in New York City with her husband and two children. **Suzanne Oliver** has worked as a writer and editor and graduated from Texas Christian University and lives in New York City and Jaffrey Center, New Hampshire, with her husband and three children. **Priscilla Warner**, a graduate of the University of Pennsylvania, she worked as an art director at various advertising agencies in Boston and New York. She lives with her family in a suburb of New York City.

1. How did the book's format (a three-way memoir written in first person) contribute to the overall feel of the book? At what points did the women write different versions of the same event? How does each woman's individual prejudices and religion color her interpretations of the discussions?

2. How does each woman's role as a mother influence the direction and tone of the Faith Club? Would the club have been different if it had included mothers as well as women with no children? How did the children play a role in the challenges to each woman's faith?

3. To which woman did you most relate, and why? Was it the one you expected when you began the book? If you identified with one of the women because you share her religious beliefs, did you agree with her presentation of your faith? What did you disagree with, and why?

4. Much of the first half of the book deals with Suzanne's and Priscilla's struggles to define anti-Semitism and to confront their prejudices about the other's faith. Did you feel that Ranya was unfairly relegated to the role of "mediator," or did she welcome it? "For months, I had to bide my time patiently." Why do you think Ranya waited to bring up her own struggles with Suzanne's and Priscilla's faiths?

5. Ranya says, "The more that science unravels about the wonders of life and the universe, the more I am in awe of it." Do you think this combination of science and faith is realistic, or must one ultimately take precedence over the other?

6. How does each woman step out of her individual, cozy and homogeneous comfort zone, and in what ways does each remain there?

7. In Chapter 12, "Intimations of Mortality," the women discuss their differing views about death and the afterlife. Which understanding of death was most comforting to you? Which image of the afterlife was most comforting? Are they from the same religion?

8. When Priscilla confronts Suzanne about her confession that she was uncomfortable being mistaken for a Jew, Ranya says, "She wouldn't want to be a Muslim, either." Do you agree? Why or why not? Is Suzanne's discomfort an inevitable result of being a member of the majority, of "not [being] forced to accommodate [herself] to the culture, religion, or even friendship of minorities"?

9. How is each woman's method of prayer different? How is it similar? How do Suzanne's, Ranya's, and Priscilla's prayer styles reflect the differences and similarities in their childhoods?

THE FICTION CLASS

AUTHOR: *Susan Breen*

PUBLISHER: Plume Books, February 2008

WEBSITE: www.plumebooks.com
www.susanjbreen.com

AVAILABLE IN:
Trade Paperback, 304 pages, $14.00
ISBN: 978-0-452-28910-9

SUBJECT: Family/Relationships/
Personal Challenges (Fiction)

"The Fiction Class reminds us of what the right words in the proper order can give: pleasure, laughter, heartache, and, on rare and stunning occasions and just in the nick of time, redemption." —**Marisa de los Santos, author of Belong To Me and Love Walked In**

SUMMARY: On paper, Arabella Hicks seems more than qualified to teach her fiction class on the Upper West Side: she's a writer herself and she's passionate about books. On the other hand, she's thirty-eight, single, and has been writing the same book for the last seven years. Also, she's distracted. Her mother, ailing from Parkinson's and living in a nearby nursing home, still has enough energy in her to leave Arabella feeling angry and depleted each time she visits. When her class takes a surprising turn and her lessons start to spill over into her weekly visits, she suddenly finds she might be holding the key to her mother's love and, dare she say it, her own inspiration. *The Fiction Class* is a work of wit and intelligence with a hefty emotional weight.

ABOUT THE AUTHOR: **Susan Breen** teaches fiction classes for Gotham Writers' Workshop in Manhattan. Her short stories have been published by a number of literary magazines, among them *American Literary Review* and *North Dakota Quarterly*. She is also a contributor to *The Writer* and *Writers' Digest*. She lives in Irvington, New York, with her husband, children, two dogs and one cat.

1. Who, out of the twelve students, surprised you the most in terms of character development? For those who have taken any kind of community workshop, discuss Breen's ability to create characters that reflect the types of people who enroll in these classes.

2. How do Arabella's class lectures and writing assignments reflect, highlight, or provide insight into her personal life? How do they work as vehicles for flashback and foreshadowing? What keeps the lecture/classroom scenes from becoming formulaic?

3. Arabella isn't always a sympathetic character. What keeps us interested in Arabella as a character? What allows us to keep reading about her until the end of the book?

4. What does her writing reveal to you about the lives of people afflicted with multiple sclerosis and Parkinson's and the lives of their caretakers?

5. Is there anything ironic about Chuck's place as the romantic hero? Does he change much in the novel, or is it simply Arabella's perspective (of him, and others) that changes?

6. How did you feel that Arabella could never answer her mother firmly about her own beliefs about God, fortune-tellers, and miracles?

7. What did Vera's story reveal—not only about her relationship with Arabella, but about her perspective before and after her husband's multiple sclerosis diagnosis?

8. Arabella says, "Theme is how you interpret the world." What would you consider to be the central themes of this book? What would Breen have you believe about familial and romantic relationships, the nature of love, and the role of faith and hope in our lives?

9. Like all good literature, *The Fiction Class* contains symbols that reinforce the theme(s) of the novel. Arabella considers various possibilities for the apple as a symbol, but how do you think it works to support the novel's thematic development? What other symbols did you notice when reading the book? What or who did these images and items symbolize?

10. The *Fiction Class* is a highly reflexive novel in that it contains or employs many of the devices Arabella talks about in her lectures. Did this make the novel more or less enjoyable to read? Did you learn anything from Arabella's lectures? Did her lectures inspire you to try writing on your own?

11. Do you think that Vera's vision of her husband (as described in Marvel's letter) qualified as a miracle? Why do you think unhappy endings—or, at the very least, endings that are neither happy nor sad—are preferred in literary fiction?

FIRST COMES LOVE, THEN COMES MALARIA

How a Peace Corps Poster Boy Won My Heart and a Third World Adventure Changed My Life

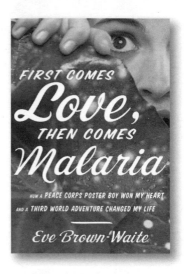

AUTHOR: *Eve Brown-Waite*

PUBLISHER: Broadway Books, April 2009

WEBSITE: www.broadwaybooks.com

AVAILABLE IN:
Hardcover, 224 pages, $23.95
ISBN: 978-0-7679-2935-6

SUBJECT: Women's Lives/Culture & World Issues/Social Issues (Memoir)

SUMMARY: Eve Brown, college diploma in hand and notions of saving the world in her head, was unsure about what to do with the rest of her life. Something noble . . . yet glamorous, she hoped. With some ambivalence she looked into joining the Peace Corps. When she fell for her dashing and altruistic Peace Corps recruiter, John, all the ambivalence disappeared. She absolutely had to join the Peace Corps, if for no other reason than to win John's heart. Off to Ecuador she went—and after a year in the jungle, back to the States she ran, vowing to stay within easy reach of a decaf cappuccino for the rest of her life. But John—now her husband—had other ideas. Before long, the couple was off to Uganda, and the fun was just beginning.

With wit and candor, *First Comes Love, then Comes Malaria* chronicles Eve's misadventures as an aspiring do-gooder. From intestinal parasites to being held hostage, from eating termites to cultural misunderstandings, here is an honest look at the search for love and purpose—from a woman who finds both in the last place she expected.

ABOUT THE AUTHOR: **Eve Brown-Waite** was a finalist for both an Iowa Review Award and a Glimmer Train Award, and the first runner up for the 2008 New Millennium Writings Award for stories she wrote about her time abroad. She lives with her husband and two children in Massachusetts.

1. Did Eve misrepresent herself to John during her Peace Corps interview? What qualities did she display at her interview and afterward that convinced him she was right for the job? Do you think he was right?

2. What do you think of John? Is the portrayal of "St. John" an honest portrait, or do you think he is an idealized character? What are his negative characteristics?

3. Despite Eve's reluctance to actually follow through with her Peace Corps plans, she handles the challenges of her Ecuadorian mission well and derives sincere pleasure from helping the orphans she works with. Do you think her initial doubts are overblown? Does her commitment surprise her? Do you think she would have gone if not for John?

4. What lessons do you think Eve learned from her time in Ecuador? Do you think her Peace Corps experience helped her prepare for life in Uganda?

5. How do Eve and John relate to the expat community in Uganda? Do they have much in common? How much do they rely on their fellow expats? Is this a good support system? Why or why not?

6. What do you make of the way Eve and John react to the very real dangers of Uganda: bombings, corruption, political unrest, and the hostage situation in their own home. Does their attitude change after the birth of their daughter?

7. Eve reasons that it's better to raise a child in a dangerous but nurturing environment rather than one that is modern and convenient but full of material distractions. Do you agree? Given the two extremes of New York and Uganda, which would you choose, and why?

8. How does Eve deal with the income disparity in Uganda? How does she adapt to the reality of having hired "help"?

9. What about Eve's AIDS prevention work? Do you think she finds her few opportunities to contribute to be a source of satisfaction, or merely frustration? Do you think she had a positive impact on her community?

10. After reading Eve's account, did your impressions of Ecuador or Uganda change? How do you think native Ecuadorians and Ugandans would react to Eve's descriptions of their countries?

11. Did the book impact your opinion of the Peace Corps and similar organizations? How do you think you would handle the challenges of living in a developing country?

GILDING LILY

AUTHOR: **Tatiana Boncompagni**

PUBLISHER: Avon A, September 2008

WEBSITE: www.avonbooks.com
www.boncompagni.net

AVAILABLE IN:
Trade Paperback, 320 pages, $13.95
ISBN: 978-0-061-45101-0

SUBJECT: Women's Lives/Identity/
Personal Discovery (Fiction)

"Boncompagni has an eye for the comedic aspects of this privileged, insular group. . . . The author's familiarity with the world she describes allows her to garnish the narrative with tantalizing details, and her protagonist is likable even at her most dastardly." —Publishers Weekly

SUMMARY: As Lily Bartholomew navigates kiddie birthday parties starring chart-topping entertainment, society dinner-dances, and vacations to exclusive hideaways with the mother-in-law from hell, she constantly wonders, "On what planet have I landed?"

After all, she's just a down-to-earth gal from suburbia who felt as if she'd landed in the middle of a fairy tale when she married Robert. Lily begins writing essays about life among the rich and snobbish, which tosses her into the spotlight and in the path of social disaster. But as Lily navigates her way through the shark-infested waters of Manhattan society, she starts to rediscover her own place in the world—and how to regain what truly matters.

ABOUT THE AUTHOR: **Tatiana Boncompagni**, 30, is a Manhattan-based freelancer for the *New York Times Sunday Styles* section and the *Financial Times* Style & Shopping pages. Her writing has also appeared in *Vogue, Cookie*, and *InStyle*. A top-ten graduate from Georgetown University's prestigious School of Foreign Service, she worked for the *Wall Street Journal* in Europe, and, later, as a reporter for the *Legal Times* in Washington, D.C. Boncompagni currently lives in New York City with her husband and two children.

1. Why do you think Lily became so upset when her mother-in-law decorated her new apartment without Lily's consent or input? How does Lily's discomfort in her own home mirror how she feels in general about her life?

2. What are your impressions of Robert? Is he a good husband? Why do you think he spends so much time with Josephine? Do you think most marriages go through periods of discord and disconnect like Lily and Robert's marriage does?

3. The majority of the socialites in the book are so mean to Lily. Why do you think Lily puts up with their cruelty for so long? Do you think she's being honest with herself about why she yearns for their acceptance?

4. Edward, Lily's father-in-law seems to enjoy it when Josephine, his wife, is put in place by Robert, and occasionally does so himself, but he fails to intercede on Lily's behalf in any meaningful way. Why doesn't he? Do you think many marriages evolve into similarly hateful unions?

5. While in St. Bart's, Lily runs into a woman who tells her that women get either fat or bitter as they age. Do you think this is true? Why do you think some women feel like they only have these two choices in life?

6. Fashion is an important aspect of the book. What does it represent to Lily? And what does it say about her character? What do you think the author is trying to say about our cultural obsession with clothes, handbags and shoes?

7. Do you think Lily was justified in moving forward with the article about Emily Leiberwaller? Would you have made the same choice or handled the aftermath of the article's publication similarly? If not, what would you have done differently?

8. Discuss the scene in the jewelry store bathroom with Christian de Rambouillet. What does it foreshadow?

9. What does Lily learn about herself and how does she grow over the course of the novel? What do you think her biggest errors in judgment were? How does she redeem herself?

10. The author Tatiana Boncompagni was inspired by Edith Wharton's *House of Mirth* when writing *Gilding Lily*. What similarities in theme and subject matter do you see between Boncompagni's work and that of Wharton? Are there parallels between the time that Wharton was writing and now?

GIRLS OF RIYADH

AUTHOR: *Rajaa Alsanea*
Marilyn Booth, Translator

PUBLISHER: Penguin Books, June 2008
(Reprint Edition)

WEBSITE: www.penguin.com

AVAILABLE IN:
Trade Paperback, 304 pages, $14.00
ISBN: 978-0-143-11347-8

SUBJECT: Culture & World Issues/
Relationships/Women's Lives (Fiction)

"*The daring debut by a young Saudi Arabian woman—imagine* Sex and the City, *if the city in question were Riyadh.*" —*Time*

"*[The] work of a brave, intelligent young woman. One of those rare books with the power to shake up an entrenched society.*" —*Los Angeles Times*

"*A taboo-breaking novel.*" —*The Washington Post*

"*A rare glimpse into ordinary life for young women in Saudi Arabia.*" —*San Francisco Chronicle*

SUMMARY: When Rajaa Alsanea boldly chose to open up the hidden world of Saudi women—their private lives and their conflicts with the traditions of their culture—she caused a sensation across the Arab world. Now in English, Alsanea's tale of the personal struggles of four young upper-class women offers Westerners an unprecedented glimpse into a society often veiled from view. Living in restrictive Riyadh but traveling all over the globe, these modern Saudi women literally and figuratively shed traditional garb as they search for love, fulfillment, and their place somewhere in between Western society and their Islamic home.

ABOUT THE AUTHOR: **Rajaa Alsanea** grew up in Riyadh, Saudi Arabia, the daughter of a family of doctors. She currently lives in Chicago where she is a dental graduate student. She is twenty-five years old, and this is her first novel.

1. Gamrah's mother believes that "woman is to man as butter is to sun." Do all the men in this novel have a corrupting influence on the women who love them?

2. In what ways are Michelle, Gamrah, Lamees, and Sadeem restricted by tradition and how do they work around it?

3. This story of young women looking for love has been compared to books like *Bridget Jones's Diary* and *Sex and the City*. In what ways does *Girls of Riyadh's* geographic and social context set it apart from its Western counterparts?

4. When she discovers her husband's secrets, Gamrah desperately attempts to hold her marriage together. Do you think she is a victim of circumstance, or is she guilty of dishonesty in her own right?

5. What role does the widow Um Nuwayyir play for the girls? Is she a positive or negative model for them?

6. What are Michelle, Sadeem, Gamrah, and Lamees's individual relationships to religion and religious law? How do they differ?

7. After a couple of romantic disappointments, Michelle realizes she can never replace her true love with another man. Do you agree with this conclusion, and do you view her ending as a happy one?

8. Does this novel have a moral point of view and if so, what is it?

9. During the scene where Lamees graduates from medical school, the narrator describes her joy of "having it all": love, a career, a new baby on the way. How did Lamees manage to pull off this feat—was it skill or simply luck?

10. The narrator says early on that every one of her friends "lives huddled in the shadow of a man, or a wall, or a man who is a wall." Is this true for all of the characters, and is it true even at the end of the story?

HANNAH'S DREAM

AUTHOR: *Diane Hammond*

PUBLISHER: Harper Paperbacks
September 2008

WEBSITE: www.harpercollins.com
www.dianehammond.com

AVAILABLE IN:
Trade Paperback, 336 pages, $13.95
ISBN: 978-0-061-56825-1

SUBJECT: Identity/Relationships/Nature
(Fiction)

"Hammond's language is spare and beautiful." —Seattle Times

"Hammond [writes] clean prose, pitch-perfect dialogue, and [has a] keen eye for social detail." —Boston Globe

"Hammond is a gifted writer, and the descriptions she uses get to something deep within a character in a few words." —Portland Oregonian

SUMMARY: For 41years, Samson Brown has been caring for Hannah, the lone elephant at the down-at-heel Max L. Biedelman Zoo. Having vowed not to retire until an equally loving and devoted caretaker is found to replace him, Sam rejoices when smart, compassionate Neva Wilson is hired as the new elephant keeper. But Neva quickly discovers what Sam already knows: that despite their loving care, Hannah is isolated from other elephants, and her feet are nearly ruined from standing on hard concrete all day. Using her contacts in the zookeeping world, Neva and Sam hatch a plan to send Hannah to an elephant sanctuary—just as the zoo's angry, unhappy director launches an aggressive revitalization campaign that spotlights Hannah as the star attraction, inextricably tying Hannah's future to the fate of the Max L. Biedelman Zoo. A charming and captivating novel certain to enthrall readers of *Water for Elephants*, *Hannah's Dream* is a beautifully told tale rich in heart, humor, and intelligence.

ABOUT THE AUTHOR: **Diane Hammond**, the author of two previous novels, *Going to Bend* and *Homesick Creek*, is the recipient of an Oregon Arts Commission literary fellowship and served as a spokesperson for the Free Willy Keiko Foundation and the Oregon Coast Aquarium. She lives in Bend, Oregon, with her husband and daughter.

1. Several characters in *Hannah's Dream* have or are given mixed, scrambled or multiple identities. Harriet, for instance, takes on the persona of Max Biedelman. Which other characters have identity issues, and why?

2. Sam and Max Biedelman develop a deep friendship. On what do the uneducated black zookeeper and worldly old woman base their relationship? Would their relationship be different if they had met today? Or under different circumstances?

3. Animals both large and small play key roles in the lives of the characters in *Hannah's Dream*. Why are they so important to their owners and keepers? In what ways are the various animal/human relationships similar, and in what what ways are they different?

4. Why, at the end of the book, does Corinna begin to re-examine her relationship with God?

5. Will Sam and Corinna ever travel to the Pachyderm Sanctuary to visit Hannah?

6. Every character in this book (with the possible exception of Johnson Johnson) has been permanently altered or even defined by one essential event, calamity or crisis. In what ways do these personal histories allow the various characters to understand, and sympathize with, other characters—even if their secrets remain secret?

7. Harriet Saul is initially portrayed as the villain in *Hannah's Dream*, but does she deserve it? Did she change over the course of the book, and if so, how? Why?

8. What's the deal with Johnson Johnson? Is he a savant, a fool, or a genius?

9. Sam and Corinna treat Hannah as the reincarnation of their stillborn daughter. Do they mean this literally or figuratively?

10. Neva Wilson describes Hannah as a "charismatic mega-vertebrate," a description that also includes whales, dolphins and other large and popular mammals. Do these animals have a place in today's zoos? Why?

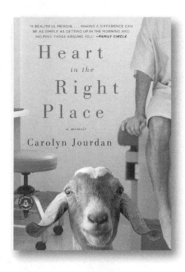

HEART IN THE RIGHT PLACE

AUTHOR: *Carolyn Jourdan*

PUBLISHER: Algonquin Books, August 2008

WEBSITE: www.algonquin.com
www.carolynjourdan.com

AVAILABLE IN:
Trade Paperback, 320 pages, $14.95
ISBN: 978-1-56512-613-8

SUBJECT: Family/Personal Discovery/
Inspiration (Memoir)

"[A]n absolute delight of a book: warm, funny and written with great heart and understanding." —**Howard Shirley, *BookPage***

"Former U.S. Senate counsel Jourdan writes of giving up her fast-paced life in Washington to work in her father's family medical practice office in east Tennessee. . . . Jourdan's dispatches from the reception desk make for a stirring, beautiful memoir that is alternately hilarious and heartbreaking, and ultimately a triumph." —***Publishers Weekly*** **(starred review)**

"A beautiful memoir. . . . Making a difference can be as simple as getting up in the morning and helping those around you." —***Family Circle***

SUMMARY: Carolyn Jourdan, an attorney on Capitol Hill, thought she had it made. But when her mother has a heart attack, she returns home—to the Tennessee mountains, where her father is a country doctor and her mother works as his receptionist. Jourdan offers to fill in for her mother until she gets better. But days turn into weeks as she trades her suits for scrubs. Most important, though, she comes to understand what her caring and patient father means to her close-knit community. With great humor and great tenderness, *Heart in the Right Place* shows that some of our biggest heroes are the ones living right beside us.

ABOUT THE AUTHOR: **Carolyn Jourdan**, a former U.S. Senate Counsel to the Committee on Environment and Public Works and the Committee on Governmental Affairs (now Homeland Security and Governmental Affairs), is an award-winning writer and documentary filmmaker. She lives on the family farm in east Knox County, Tennessee.

1. Carolyn Jourdan must leave her glamorous, fast-paced life in Washington, D.C., in order to return to her small hometown to help her parents. What kinds of sacrifices have you made for your family? In what ways did those sacrifices affect your life? Were you, like the author, surprised by how you were changed by them?

2. What are the trade-offs in being a small-town doctor versus being a doctor in the big city? What is gained and lost on both sides? What would we lose if small-town doctors disappeared?

3. Have you ever been in a situation where you were the only person who could help, and if so, how did you manage it?

4. How would you characterize Carolyn Jourdan's relationship with her father? In what ways is it similar to or different from her relationship with her mother?

5. During one of her telephone conversations with Jacob, the author says, "You know how we always talk about wanting to be in public service so we can help people. . . . Well, in this place I feel sometimes like I really am helping people. Actual people. It's not just an idea. I can't help them much. I know it's not glamorous, but sometimes I think maybe I'm doing more good swabbing up body fluids and being a friendly face here than I ever did working in the Senate." Discuss the different ways people help each other. How do you think caring for others informs who you are? Share an experience you had directly assisting someone.

6. Discuss the ways in which Carolyn Jourdan's view of her father and mother shifts over the year. For instance, early on she describes them as "stoic" and "utterly self-contained." How does she see them by the end of the book?

7. When the author catches a glimpse of a human heart during surgery, she says to Henry, "If that's the heart, I gotta say, it don't look like much." Henry smiles and says, "A lot of the most important things in life 'don't look like much.'" Can you think of other examples in the book for which this holds true? Does this statement reflect a situation you have experienced?

8. Near the end of the book, the author realizes the true significance of the story about performing surgery with a pocketknife: "I'd always thought the story was about the astounding surgery. But it wasn't. It was about using the talents you had, whatever they might be, to the most constructive purpose." Who else mirrors this sentiment and why? Historical figures? People in your own life? To what degree is this true for yourself?

HOME TO HOLLY SPRINGS

AUTHOR: *Jan Karon*

PUBLISHER: Penguin Books, October 2008

WEBSITE: www.penguin.com
www.mitfordbooks.com

AVAILABLE IN:
Trade Paperback, 368 pages, $13.95
ISBN: 978-0-143-11439-0

SUBJECT: Family/Faith/Social Issues
(Fiction)

"Far from Mitford and his beloved wife Cynthia, Father Tim Kavanagh enters unfamiliar emotional territory in the town of his birth. When he receives a letter postmarked Holly Springs, Miss., that contains a cryptic two-word message written in a precise, old-fashioned hand, Father Tim decides to answer its call and return to his birthplace for the first time in 38 years. . . . Who is trying to contact him, and why? . . . In this setting away from home, we see Father Tim in a new light as he wrestles with his past and explores the origins of his religious convictions. The saga veers into magical theater as Karon (Cynthia Coppersmith's Violet Comes to Stay, *2006, etc.) ties up every loose end in Tim's past. But readers who miss Mitford's colorful eccentrics will be satisfied by Holly Springs's ample supply of quirky characters. Karon's deft interweaving of past and present infuses the Mitford saga with new energy." —Kirkus Reviews*

SUMMARY: Now, Jan Karon enchants us with the story of the newly retired priest's spur-of-the-moment adventure. For the first time in decades, Father Tim returns to his birthplace, Holly Springs, Mississippi, in response to a mysterious, unsigned note saying simply: *"Come home."* Little does he know how much these two words will change his life. A story of long-buried secrets, forgiveness, and the wonder of discovering new people, places, and depth of feeling, *Home to Holly Springs* will enthrall new readers and longtime fans alike.

ABOUT THE AUTHOR: **Jan Karon** is the author of the bestselling series of Mitford novels.

1. Which of the two men, Jim Houck or Father Tim, do you think benefited more from the truth about what happened between their fathers: Father Tim learning the truth about what happened or Jim finally being able to tell him the truth?

2. What do you think Matthew Kavanagh's last words meant?

3. Father Tim is surprised that the courthouse was as large as he remembered it. Discuss times you revisited places from your childhood only to discover that things were different than you recalled.

4. When young Timothy Kavanagh uses a racist epithet, he's told to read First Corinthians 12:13, which says, "For we were all baptized by one Spirit into one body—whether Jews or Greeks, slave or free—and we were all given the one Spirit to drink." How do you think it was so easy for people to profess their Christianity while still embracing racism?

5. Father Tim reflects that since returning to Holly Springs, "his own bear had lumbered up to the wagon." Discuss what he meant. With what other bears are the characters in this book struggling?

6. Discuss the instances in *Home to Holly Springs* where the sins of the father are passed on to the son. Father Tim's father was a distant and strict person prone to bouts of depression. Why do you think Father Tim's parenting style wasn't negatively affected by how his father treated him?

7. Father Tim wanted to ask his dad, "Why do you hate me?" How do you think he would have reacted if the question had been posed?

8. As in Jan Karon's previous novels, food and fellowship go hand in hand. Discuss a few examples in the book where events and people are directly tied to food. What are the foods that you associate with childhood memories or other specific times in your life? Have you carried on those traditions?

9. Several people in the book say it's a must to see Graceland before one dies. What are your must-visit destinations?

10. Do you think the favor Peggy asks of Father Tim is selfish? What would you have done if you were in Father Tim's shoes?

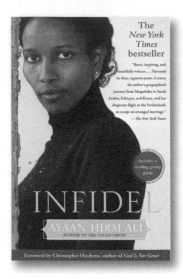

INFIDEL

AUTHOR: *Ayaan Hirsi Ali*

PUBLISHER: Free Press, April 2008

WEBSITE: www.simonsays.com

AVAILABLE IN:
Trade Paperback, 384 pages, $15.00
ISBN: 978-0-743-28969-6

SUBJECT: Culture & World Issues/Faith/ Women's Lives (Memoir)

"Ayaan Hirsi Ali is one of Europe's most controversial political figures and a target for terrorists. A notably enigmatic personality whose fierce criticisms of Islam have made her a darling of . . . conservatives . . . and . . . popular with leftists. . . . Soft-spoken but passionate." —**The Boston Globe**

"Too potent a social critic to be tolerated any longer [in her home country] . . . an unflinching advocate of women's rights and an unflinching critic of Islamic extremism." —**The New York Times**

SUMMARY: In this profoundly affecting memoir from the internationally renowned author of *The Caged Virgin*, Ayaan Hirsi Ali tells her astonishing life story, from her traditional Muslim childhood in Somalia, Saudi Arabia, and Kenya, to her intellectual awakening and activism in the Netherlands, and her current life under armed guard in the West.

Ultimately a celebration of triumph over adversity, Hirsi Ali's story tells how a bright little girl evolved out of dutiful obedience to become an outspoken, pioneering freedom fighter. As Western governments struggle to balance democratic ideals with religious pressures, no story could be timelier or more significant.

ABOUT THE AUTHOR: **Ayaan Hirsi Ali** was born in Mogadishu, Somalia, was raised Muslim, and spent her childhood and young adulthood in Africa and Saudi Arabia. In 1992, Hirsi Ali came to the Netherlands as a refugee, earned her college degree in political science, denounced Islam after the September 11 terrorist attacks, and served as a Dutch parliamentarian, fighting for the rights of Muslim women in Europe, the enlightenment of Islam, and security in the West. She now lives in the U.S.

1. Hirsi Ali tells us that this book is "the story of what I have experienced, what I have seen, and why I think the way I do." Which experiences does she highlight as being integral to forming her current views on Islam?
2. What significant differences between the West and Islamic Africa did she observe during her first days in Europe? Upon arriving in Holland, what were her initial impressions of the Dutch people and the Dutch government? Did these change significantly as she lived there?
3. How did Hirsi Ali's immigration experience and integration into Dutch society differ from those of other Somalians?
4. Discuss the differences that Hirsi Ali noticed between raising children in Muslim countries and raising children in the West. In particular, what did she notice about Johanna's parenting? How were Muslim parents different from Dutch parents in their instructions to their children on the playground?
5. In Hirsi Ali's words, "A Muslim girl does not make her own decisions or seek control. She is trained to be docile. If you are a Muslim girl, you disappear, until there is almost no you inside you." How do the three generations of women in Hirsi Ali's family differ in their willingness to "submit" to this doctrine?
6. As seen through Hirsi Ali's eyes, what factors contributed to Haweya's death? How might members of her family describe events differently?
7. Although Hirsi Ali mostly refrains from criticizing her father, she publishes the personal letter he wrote her upon her divorce. Why do you think she included this letter? Were you surprised by any other intimate details of her life that she revealed in the book?
8. The events of September 11th caused Hirsi Ali to reread sections of the Quran and to evaluate the role of violence in Islam. Consequently, her interpretation of September 11th differs from those around her. What does she conclude? Do you agree with her analysis?
9. Hirsi Ali lists three goals she wished to accomplish by joining Parliament. By the book's end has she accomplished all three? How did her views of the Dutch government change over time?
10. Examine Hirsi Ali's relationship with her brother. How did Mahad's and Abeh's reactions to her political work differ?
11. Throughout her political career, Hirsi Ali has made several bold statements challenging the Muslim world. In your opinion, were these declarations worth the risk?
12. Has this book changed the way you view Islam? According to Hirsi Ali, is Islam compatible with Western values and culture? Do you agree with her?

IN HOVERING FLIGHT

AUTHOR: *Joyce Hinnefeld*

PUBLISHER: Unbridled Books
September 2008

WEBSITE: www.unbridledbooks.com

AVAILABLE IN:
Hardcover, 288 pages, $24.95
ISBN: 978-1-932961-58-4

SUBJECT: Family/Relationships/Art
(Fiction)

"A provocative and page-turning debut novel. . . . Hinnefeld's drama soars."
—Publishers Weekly

"Joyce Hinnefeld is a gifted and wise storyteller who—through many layers—reveals the core of each character. In Hovering Flight *is a compelling and mysterious novel."* —**Ursula Hegi**

"As glorious and beautiful and fleeting as the birdsong." —**Michael Fraser, Joseph Beth Booksellers**

"I loved everything about it." —**Nancy Olson, Quail Ridge Books & Music**

SUMMARY: At 34, Scarlet Kavanagh has the kind of homecoming no child wishes, a visit back to family and dear friends for the gentle passing of her mother, Addie, a famous bird artist and an even more infamous environmental activist. Though Addie and her husband, ornithologist Tom Kavanagh, have made their life in southeastern Pennsylvania, Addie has chosen to die at the New Jersey home of her dearest friend, Cora. Now, in their final moments together, Scarlet hopes to put to rest the last tensions that have marked their relationship. Scarlet slowly comes to peace with her mother's complicated life. But she can do the same with her own? Scarlet has carried a secret into these foggy days—a secret for Addie, one that involves Cora, too.

ABOUT THE AUTHOR: **Joyce Hinnefeld** is an Associate Professor of Writing at Moravian College in Bethlehem, Pennsylvania. She is the author of a short story collection, *Tell Me Everything and Other Stories*, which was awarded the 1997 Breadloaf Writer's Conference Bakeless Prize in fiction in 1997. *In Hovering Flight* is her first novel.

1. What was your immediate response to this novel? Is there anything in your personal experience or of anyone you know that is similar to what happens in the novel, such as the untimely death of a parent, or having longtime close friendships similar to those in the novel? A love of nature and bird song? Or a strong interest or activism in a particular area of interest? If so, how did that affect your reading of the novel?

2. How would you describe the tone and style of this novel? What did you enjoy most about the novel? What did you have problems with, if anything? Why?

3. Two statements expressive of the differing points of view on this issue that you might be acquainted with are the old dictum, "Art for art's sake," on the one hand, and Ezra Pound's admonition—"All Art is didactic"—on the other. What do you think this novel is saying about that debate? If you came to this novel with a strong position or opinion about the relationship between Art and Politics, how, if at all, did it affect your reading of this novel? Do you agree with Addie's assessment of herself as an artist at the end of the book?

4. What major themes can you identify in the novel? How do you come to your conclusions?

5. How would you describe the portrait of family life, marriage, and friendship as presented in this novel? Whose story is it, do you think? What about the characters in the novel? How do we learn about each of them? The author says her favorite is Tom. Which is yours, and why? Which is your least favorite, and why? With respect to Addie, does your opinion of her change over the course of the novel? If so, why? If not, why not?

6. Birds: What about them, in this novel? How many and in what ways can you find that the author uses birds and bird song as symbols, or metaphors, in this novel or to carry the narrative? Do you believe that Addie ever really saw the Cuvier's Kinglet? What does it symbolize, if anything, to you?

7. How did or did not the inclusion of the events of 9/11 affect your reading of the novel? Why? How well, or not, do you think the author handled this part of the narrative?

8. Would you recommend this novel to a friend to read? Why? If not, why not?

INTERRED WITH THEIR BONES

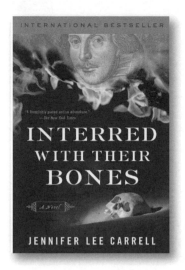

AUTHOR: *Jennifer Lee Carrell*

PUBLISHER: Plume Books, August 2008

WEBSITE: www.plumebooks.com
www.jenniferleecarrell.com

AVAILABLE IN:
Trade Paperback, 432 pages, $15.00
ISBN: 978-0-452-28989-5

SUBJECT: History/Adventure/Intrigue
(Fiction)

"[A] smart . . . notable debut literary thriller." —USA Today

"This debut mystery kicks off with quite a bang . . . the author never lets her pace sag as the story's roots reach back to Shakepeare's time. High-class fun." —Newsweek

"Plot twists worthy of The Da Vinci Code.*" —**Publishers Weekly** (starred review)*

SUMMARY: *Interred with Their Bones* introduces readers to the cryptic and fascinating world of "occult" Shakespeare, the study of the word games, puzzles and ciphers found all throughout the Bard's works. The action begins on the eve of the Globe's production of *Hamlet* when Shakespeare scholar and theater director Kate Stanley's eccentric mentor Rosalind Howard gives her a mysterious box, claiming to have made a ground-breaking discovery. Before she can reveal it to Kate, the Globe is burned to the ground and Roz is found dead . . . murdered precisely in the manner of Hamlet's father. Inside the box, Kate finds the first piece in a Shake-spearean puzzle, setting her on a deadly, high stakes treasure hunt. From London to Harvard to the American West, Kate races to evade a killer and to solve a tantalizing string of clues hidden in the words of Shakespeare, which may unlock one of history's greatest secrets.

ABOUT THE AUTHOR: **Jennifer Lee Carrell** holds a Ph.D. in English and American literature from Harvard University and is the author of *The Speckled Monster: A Historical Tale of Battling Smallpox*. In addition to writing for *Smithsonian* magazine, Carrell has taught in the history and literature program at Harvard and directed Shakespeare for Harvard's Hyperion Theatre Company. She lives in Tucson, Arizona.

1. One of the pervading themes of *Interred with Their Bones* is the gap between the academic and the practical when it comes to the works of Shakespeare. The great gap between Roz Howard's "ivory tower" approach to Shakespeare and Kate Stanley's need to have the actual hands-on experience of directing a Shakespearean play provides the opening conflict of the novel. When it comes to classic theater, is studying the plays and the playwright enough? Is it important to experience Shakespeare's works in the way the playwright intended—performed before a live audience?

2. In Chapter Two, Sir Henry makes the comment: "A secret is a kind of promise. It can also be a prison." What does he mean by this? Is he trying to subconsciously give Kate a message about his own future actions?

3. One of the more fascinating characters of the novel isn't a person at all; rather, it is a book, Shakespeare's First Folio collection. How does the author use this book to lay the framework for the rest of the novel?

4. The title of the book comes from a quotation by Shakespeare: "The evil that men do lives after them; The good is oft interred with their bones." How does this still hold true today? Why do we so often remember the names of criminals, but not the names of those who capture them?

5. Throughout the novel, a number of different theories emerge about the identities of possible alternate authors of Shakespeare's work. If it was ever proven that Shakespeare did *not* actually write his own plays, would it lessen the importance of those plays?

6. Shakespeare's lost play is the equivalent of the Holy Grail for Kate. She seems to place the utmost importance on discovering it over all else. Do you share, or understand, her feelings about the play? What kind of artifact would be your Holy Grail?

7. The killer recreates murder scenes from some of Shakespeare's most famous plays. What is the significance of this and why?

8. In his own time, Shakespeare was considered lowbrow, an entertainer who pandered to the lower classes; time has since proven his critics wrong. Are there novelists and playwrights living today who may one day be considered the "new Shakespeare"?

9. One of the more fascinating details revealed in the book is Shakespeare's unusual influence throughout the American West. Why do you think the pioneers and cowboys were drawn to Shakespeare? What purpose did Shakespeare's works serve in their lives?

IN THE WOODS

AUTHOR: *Tana French*

PUBLISHER: Penguin Books, May 2008

WEBSITE: www.penguin.com

AVAILABLE IN:
Trade Paperback, 464 pages, $14.00
ISBN: 978-0-143-11349-2

SUBJECT: Intrigue/Personal Challenges/
Relationships (Fiction)

"Readers who like their hardboiled police procedurals with an international flair will love Irish author Tana French's debut novel. . . . In The Woods *is as creepily imaginative as it gets."* —*USA Today*

"Tana French promises two whodunits for the price of one in her harrowing first novel. Drawn by the grim nature of her plot and the lyrical ferocity of her writing, even smart people who should know better will be able to lose themselves in these dark woods." —**Marilyn Stasio,** *The New York Times Book Review*

"[In The Woods] plies dark, shuddery suspense to the breaking point . . . [a] thoroughly taunting suspense novel." —*New York Daily News*

SUMMARY: In a small Dublin suburb in the summer of 1984, three children do not return from the dark and silent woods. When the police arrive, they find only one of the children gripping a tree trunk in terror, wearing blood-filled sneakers, and unable to recall a single detail of the previous hours. Twenty years later, the found boy, Rob Ryan, is a detective on the Dublin Murder Squad and keeps his past a secret. But when a twelve-year-old girl is found murdered in the same woods, he and Detective Cassie Maddox—his partner and closest friend—find themselves investigating a case chillingly similar to the previous unsolved mystery. Ryan has the chance to uncover both the mystery of the case before him and that of his own shadowy past. Richly atmospheric, stunning in its complexity, and surprising to the end, this book is sure to enthrall fans of *Mystic River* and *The Lovely Bones*.

ABOUT THE AUTHOR: **Tana French** grew up in Ireland, Italy, the United States, and Malawi and has lived in Dublin since 1990. *In the Woods* is her first book. Her second novel, *The Likeness*, was released June 2008.

1. What do the woods represent symbolically in Tana French's novel? Does their significance change as the story progresses?

2. The loss or absence of stable families is a recurring motif in *In the Woods*. How do French's characters, particularly Ryan, attempt to compensate for this absence?

3. Does the Irish setting of *In the Woods* contribute significantly to the telling of the story, or do you find French's novel to be about humanity on a more universal level?

4. How does Ryan's experience in the woods at the age of twelve affect his ability to function as a detective? Is it always a hindrance to him, or are there ways in which it improves and deepens his insights?

5. Cassie Maddox, Ryan's partner, is perhaps the most consistently appealing character in the novel. What are her most attractive qualities? What are the weaker points of her personality? Does Ryan ever fully appreciate her?

6. After sleeping together, Ryan and Cassie cease to be friends. Why do you think the experience of physical intimacy is so damaging to their relationship? Are there other reasons why their friendship falls apart?

7. Ryan states that he both craves truth and tells lies. How reliable to you find him as a narrator? In what ways does the theme of truth and misrepresentation lie at the heart of *In the Woods*?

8. Imagine that you are Ryan's therapist. With what aspects of his personality would you most want to help him come to terms? Do you think there would be any way to lead him out of "the woods?"

9. How convincing is French's explanation of the motivating forces that lead to Katy's murder—forces that come close to a definition of pure evil? Are such events and motivations ever truly explicable?

10. The plan to build the new motorway, trampling as it does on a past that some regard as sacred, is an outrage to the archaeologists who are trying to preserve an ancient legacy. How does this conflict fit thematically with Ryan's own contradictory desires to unearth and to pave over his past?

11. Do you have your own theories about the mysteries that remain unsolved at the end of *In the Woods*? What are they?

12. What were your thoughts and emotions upon finishing *In the Woods*? If this book affected you differently from other mysteries you have read, why do you think this was true?

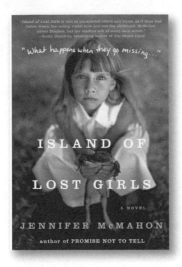

ISLAND OF LOST GIRLS

AUTHOR: *Jennifer McMahon*

PUBLISHER: Harper Paperbacks, April 2008

WEBSITE: www.harpercollins.com
www.jennifer-mcmahon.com

AVAILABLE IN:
Trade Paperback, 272 pages, $13.95
ISBN: 978-0-06-144588-0

SUBJECT: Relationships/Intrigue/
Women's Lives (Fiction)

"Like The Lovely Bones, *this book is un-put-downable from page 1. The writing is exquisite and often very funny, and the themes of childhood and loss resonate. McMahon is particularly adept at creating children, and the vibrant world of imagination where they seek a respite from reality."*
—**Boston Globe**

SUMMARY: While parked at a gas station, Rhonda sees something so incongruously surreal that at first she hardly recognizes it as a crime in progress. She watches, unmoving, as someone dressed in a rabbit costume kidnaps a young girl. Devastated over having done nothing, Rhonda joins the investigation. But the closer she comes to identifying the abductor, the nearer she gets to the troubling truth about another missing child: her best friend, Lizzy, who vanished years before.

ABOUT THE AUTHOR: **Jennifer McMahon** is the author of *Promise Not to Tell.* She grew up in suburban Connecticut, and graduated from Goddard College in 1991. Over the years, she has been a house painter, farm worker, paste-up artist, pizza delivery person, homeless shelter staff member, and has worked with mentally ill adults and children in a few different capacities. Currently, she lives in Vermont with her partner, Drea, and their daughter, Zella.

1. When the rabbit kidnaps Ernie, Rhonda finds herself unable to act because she's so completely caught off guard by what she sees. Have you ever been so surprised (or overcome with any emotion) you were paralyzed?

2. *Island of Lost Girls* moves back and forth through time, essentially following two interweaving storylines. Do you think this was an effective structure? How did it affect your reading of the book?

3. Rhonda has two love interests: Peter and Warren. How are they different? In what ways are they similar? And how does the Peter of Rhonda's youth compare to the man he is as an adult?

4. What are your observations about the different roles that fantasy, imagination, and make-believe play in the lives of both the children and adults? Do any of the characters really live in the here and now? Are these forms of escapism helpful or harmful?

5. Justine seems passive and removed but, later, Rhonda comes to believe that Justine didn't just see what was going on, but may have had a hand in hiding evidence to protect the children. Do you see her as weak or strong? A victim or a protector?

6. Daniel and Clem had been friends since boyhood. How did this affect Clem's vision of Daniel? Did it give him blind spots? And how does Rhonda's childhood friendship with Peter influence her judgment about his possible involvement in Ernie's kidnapping?

7. Ella Starkee says, "Sometimes, what a person needs most is to be forgiven." What did you think of how themes of forgiveness are played out in *Island of Lost Girls*? Are there unforgivable acts?

8. Some of the townspeople blame Trudy Florucci for Ernie's abduction, for being a "bad mother." Trudy blames Rhonda, and Rhonda blames herself. Ultimately, is there any one person at fault for what happens to Ernie? Why do you think people are so eager to find someone to take the blame?

KEEPER AND KID

AUTHOR: *Edward Hardy*

PUBLISHER: Thomas Dunne Books,
January 2008

WEBSITE: www.edwardhardy.com
www.thomasdunnebooks.com

AVAILABLE IN:
Hardcover, 304 pages, $24.95
ISBN: 978-0-312-37524-9

SUBJECT: Family/Relationships/
Identity (Fiction)

"Ed Hardy's voice in Keeper and Kid *grabs you and won't let you go until the very last page. Full of local color, bittersweet characters and a story we can all relate to—the day your past arrives on the doorstep of your present life.* Keeper and Kid *is a marvel. I dare you. Open this book and try to put it down."* —**Ann Hood, author of** *The Knitting Circle*

SUMMARY: *Keeper and Kid* is the story of what happens when a thirty-something guy, happily living his patched-together life in Providence, is yanked through the portal of parenthood and his world very nearly falls apart in the process.

In this humorous and poignant novel, Edward Hardy explores the depths of modern love, parenthood, and compromise. *Keeper and Kid* is the story of how a normal guy receives an unexpected gift and in turn must learn to ask more of others and himself. A coming-of-age story for the guy who thought he had already grown up, *Keeper and Kid* is a sharp and witty account of what we do for love.

ABOUT THE AUTHOR: **Edward Hardy** grew up in Ithaca, New York, and has an MFA from Cornell. He's the author of two novels, *Keeper and Kid* and *Geyser Life*. His short stories have appeared in over twenty magazines including: *Ploughshares, The New England Review, Prairie Schooner, Yankee,* and *The Quarterly,* and have been listed in *The Best American Short Stories*. Hardy teaches nonfiction writing at Brown. He lives outside Providence with his wife and two boys.

1. Keeper has an interesting off-beat job. How does it mesh with his personality? How does it work to advance the events in the story?

2. Keeper's life is changed overnight. What has he lost?

3. "I guess I'm not the person I thought I was." Why does Keeper say this?

4. Is Leah's reaction to Leo's arrival realistic? Does it echo anyone else's reaction to a new and disturbing situation?

5. What part do animals play in the story?

6. Can you relate to Cynthia's keeping of such a secret? What role do secrets play in the book? What makes people give them up?

7. What role does Grace play in the story?

8. Card Night plays a role in the story too. What purposes does it serve?

9. What is the fascination with The Wilsons? Would you be as intrigued if you were at Card Night?

10. Both Keeper and Leo are trying to navigate unknown territory where they don't know the language. Are there places in the book where their voyages truly intersect?

11. Why do you think Keeper is so bad at asking for help when he needs it?

12. How does Leo's book, the one Cynthia made, help Keeper get a handle on who Leo is?

13. ". . . it looks like life has flattened out and presto, some completely cool object pops up right in front of you." Is this in any way an analogy for the story?

14. How do Keeper's parents figure into the story? Should they have appeared earlier? Why do you think they didn't?

15. The "wooing" of Leah, Keeper's plan to get her back—did it work in any way?

16. How are hospitals and injury used to advance the story?

17. What does the return of Fred foretell?

18. What does Keeper gain from the upheaval of his life?

19. Can you think of an alternative ending that would be satisfying?

20. What do you think these characters will be doing in five years?

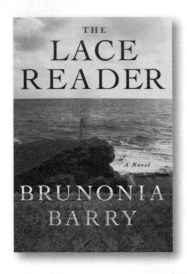

THE LACE READER

AUTHOR: **Brunonia Barry**

PUBLISHER: William Morrow, August 2008

WEBSITE: www.harpercollins.com
www.lacereader.com

AVAILABLE IN:
Hardcover, 400 pages, $24.95
ISBN: 978-0-06-162476-6

SUBJECT: Identity/Family/Relationships
(Fiction)

"With The Lace Reader, *Brunonia Barry plunges us through the looking glass and beyond to a creepy and fascinating world. Prepare to meet strange, brave, bruised, electrically alive women there. Prepare to be riveted by their story and to live under its spell long after you've reached its astonishing end."* — **Marisa de los Santos, author of** *Love Walked In* **and** *Belong to Me*

"The Lace Reader *is a page-turner, and the ending is almost as shocking as the film 'The Sixth Sense.'"* — **Salem Gazette**

SUMMARY: Towner Whitney, the self-confessed unreliable narrator of *The Lace Re*ader, hails from a family of Salem women who can read the future in the patterns in lace, and who have guarded a history of secrets going back generations, but the disappearance of two women brings Towner home to Salem and the truth about the death of her twin sister to light.

The Lace Reader is a mesmerizing tale which spirals into a world of secrets, confused identities, lies and half-truths where the reader quickly finds it's nearly impossible to separate fact from fiction, but as Towner Whitney points out early on in the novel, "There are no accidents."

ABOUT THE AUTHOR: Born and raised in Massachusetts, **Brunonia Barry** studied literature and creative writing at Green Mountain College in Vermont and at the University of New Hampshire and was one of the founding members of the Portland Stage Company. Barry lives in Salem, Massachusetts, with her husband and their beloved Golden Retriever named Byzantium.

1. For centuries, women have used lace as an adornment for their clothes and as a decoration for their homes. Just a small piece of lace on a sleeve could evoke a sense of luxury, beauty, and elegance. How does your family use lace today?

2. Have any pieces of lace been passed down to you or someone else in your family? If so, what feelings do you associate with these heirloom pieces of lace?

3. The author states that *The Lace Reader* is, at its core, about perception vs. reality. How does Rafferty's perception of Towner color his judgment of what she says and does? What about Rafferty's perception of Cal and his actions?

4. At the very start of *The Lace Reader*, Towner Whitney, the protagonist, tells the reader that she's a liar and that she's crazy. By the end of the book do you agree with her?

5. Eva reveals that she speaks in cliché so that her words do not influence the choices made by the recipients of her lace reading sessions. Do you think that's possible? Can a cliche be so over used that it loses its original meaning?

6. The handmade-lace industry of Ipswich quickly vanished when lace making machines were introduced. At that same moment, the economic freedom of the women making the handmade lace also evaporated. Why do you think that these women didn't update their business, buy the machines, and own a significant portion of the new lace making industry?

7. Do you think that May's revival of the craft of handmade lace with the abused women on Yellow Dog Island is purely symbolic or could it be, in some way, very practical?

8. What role does religion play in the novel? Is there a difference between spirituality and religion? Between faith and blind faith?

9. Towner has a special bond with the dogs of Yellow Dog Island. Do you agree that people and animals can relate to each other in extraordinary ways?

10. How do the excerpts from *The Lace Reader's Guide* and Towner's journal function in the novel? Did you use the clues in the *Guide* to help you understand the rest of the book?

11. How much does family history influence who a person becomes? Do you believe that certain traits or talents are genetic and can be inherited?

12. If you could learn to read lace and see things about your future, would you?

THE LAST CHINESE CHEF

AUTHOR: *Nicole Mones*

PUBLISHER: Mariner Books, May 2008

WEBSITE: www.nicolemones.com
www.marinerbooks.com

AVAILABLE IN:
Trade Paperback, 228 pages, $13.95
ISBN: 978-0-547-05373-8

SUBJECT: Relationships/Culture & World
Issues/Personal Discovery (Fiction)

"Mones, a contributor to Gourmet, *paints a stunning picture of a country caught between tradition and modern life. But her descriptions of Sam's adventurous Chinese recipes are what will really make your mouth water. Grade: A-" —Entertainment Weekly*

SUMMARY: Nicole Mones transports readers to the fascinating world of elite cuisine in modern China with the story of an American food writer traveling in Beijing. Recently widowed Maggie MacElroy is unexpectedly called to China to settle a claim against her late husband's estate. Shocked that he may have led a secret life, she immerses herself in work as a palliative. She is sent to profile Sam, a Chinese-American who is the last in a line of gifted chefs tracing back to the Imperial Palace. As he prepares an elaborate banquet as his audition for the Cultural Olympics, Maggie learns to appreciate the beauty and balance, ritual and meaning of Chinese cooking and culture—and finds the secret ingredient that will bring solace to her heart.

ABOUT THE AUTHOR: **Nicole Mones**, the author of the *New York Times* Notable Book *Lost in Translation* and *A Cup of Light*, is a frequent contributor to Gourmet magazine. Her work, in print in eleven languages, has won the Janet Heidinger Kafka Prize for the best work of fiction by an American woman and the Pacific Northwest Booksellers Association Award. She started a textile business in China at the close of the Cultural Revolution and ran it for eighteen years before she turned to writing about that country. She lives in Portland, Oregon.

1. In the beginning of the book, Maggie has tried to deal with her husband's death shrinking "her life to a pinpoint." She disconnects from people and seems to be trying to make her world and herself smaller and smaller. When you suffered a loss in your life, did you also feel like withdrawing from the world? If you didn't, how did you feel? And if you did, how did you find your way back?

2. Maggie's trip to China is weighted with deep emotions—confusion over her late husband's possible betrayal of her, nostalgia for the time they spent in Beijing, shock, grief. What does she ultimately find therapeutic about her time there? Do you think people are generally more open to enlightening experiences when they travel? If so, how or why?

3. *The Last Chinese Chef* could be described as a novel about human healing through the lessons and joys of cuisine and the bonds between people. Several readers have written to say they felt a healing echo in themselves from reading the novel. Did you sense any of this yourself? How did the book affect you?

4. As the book illuminates China's gastronomical philosophy, we learn that Chinese cuisine is not only about fine ingredients and unique skills; it is also about *guanxi*, or relationship. Is *guanxi* a concept that is solely Chinese, or do other cultures honor connections and relationships in the same way—through food? What does Chinese food teach Maggie about *guanxi*? What did you learn that might change the way you dine and eat?

5. Sam's relationship with his father is complex and strained at times. Why has the elder Liang made the choices he has, and how have his choices contributed to the relationship with his son? Do you empathize with his decisions?

6. What is the significance of the book-within-the-novel, Sam's grandfather's work, *The Last Chinese Chef*? What deeper cultural understanding do the translated excerpts offer to Maggie, and to you as a reader?

7. When Maggie first learns about Gao Lan she is not disposed to feel friendly, yet as she gets to know the full story—slowly—her perspective on Gao Lan changes. Do you sympathize with the shift in Maggie's attitude toward this woman? Has this ever happened to you? Have you ever started out against someone and then, as you got to know more about the person, slowly changed your view?

THE LAST COWGIRL

AUTHOR: *Jana Richman*

PUBLISHER: Avon A, January 2009

WEBSITE: www.avonbooks.com

AVAILABLE IN:
Trade Paperback, 320 pages, $13.95
ISBN: 978-0-061-25719-3

SUBJECT: Personal Discovery/
Family/Regional (Fiction)

*"Richman's mastery of the emotional geography is illuminating and calls to mind the work of Pat Conroy." — **Kirkus Reviews***

*"A warm story of good folks who make bad decisions and then have to live with them." —**Publishers Weekly***

*"Readers will be irrevocably drawn into this top-notch fictional debut from an amazing new talent." —**Booklist***

SUMMARY: Dickie Sinfield's father had a dream: to be a real cowboy—an overpowering desire that propelled him to uproot his three children from their comfortable suburban cocoon and replant them on a dusty Utah ranch. Suddenly the young Dickie found herself herding cattle, attending rodeos, and wearing snap-button shirts. Proclaiming her disdain for this new life, Dickie refused to admit that deep down it suited her. But that was long ago, and now Dickie is as far from the ranch as possible. Trading in cattle round ups for traffic jams, cowboy boots for heels, she's become a successful journalist in Salt Lake City. Thanks to willful forgetfulness, she's put the experience of the ranch behind her, until a family funeral pulls her back into her old world. As hard as she tries to deny it, a cowboy heart beats strong inside this big city girl, and now she must face both the past and some big decisions about her future.

ABOUT THE AUTHOR: **Jana Richman** is the author of *Riding in the Shadows of Saints: One Woman's Story of Motorcycling the Mormon Trail*. She lives in Salt Lake City, UT.

1. The death of Dickie's brother, Heber, sets off a chain reaction in Dickie's life. Why would Heber's death trigger such a strong reaction from Dickie when the death of her mother, Ruth, did not? Would Dickie have returned to Clayton if Heber hadn't died?

2. Throughout her life Dickie's relationships with other women have been complex. How did Dickie's friendship with Holly shape her life and her decisions? How would you describe the relationship between Bev and Dickie? At one point Bev says to Dickie, "You often step aside when you ought to be stepping up." What does she mean by this?

3. "I'm very near the edge of living life in the abyss between my mother's sadness and my father's stubbornness." What does Dickie mean by this? How are pieces of Ruth and George portrayed in Dickie? In all their children?

4. The landscape in the novel is vividly rendered and it plays an important role—almost like an additional character. Each character also has a complex relationship with the Utah countryside. How have their lives, particularly Dickie's, been shaped by the land, or by a separation from it? Could Stumpy ever be separated from the place? In other words, could Stumpy have moved into Salt Lake City and lived happily with Dickie?

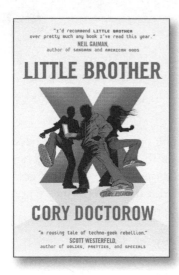

LITTLE BROTHER

AUTHOR: *Cory Doctorow*

PUBLISHER: Tor, May 2008

WEBSITE: www.tor-forge.com

AVAILABLE IN:
Hardcover, 384 pages, $17.95
ISBN: 978-0-7653-1985-2

SUBJECT: Fantasy/Adventure/Intrigue
(Fiction)

"Little Brother is generally awesome in the more vernacular sense: It's pretty freaking cool ... a fluid, instantly ingratiating fiction writer ... he's also terrific at finding the human aura shimmering around technology."
—*The Los Angeles Times*

SUMMARY: Marcus, a.k.a "w1n5t0n," is only seventeen years old, but he figures he already knows how the system works—and how to work the system. Smart, fast, and wise to the ways of the networked world, he has no trouble outwitting his high school's intrusive but clumsy surveillance systems. But his whole world changes when he and his friends find themselves caught in the aftermath of a major terrorist attack on San Francisco. In the wrong place at the wrong time, Marcus and his crew are apprehended by the Department of Homeland Security and whisked away to a secret prison where they're mercilessly interrogated for days. When the DHS finally releases them, Marcus discovers that his city has become a police state where every citizen is treated like a potential terrorist. He knows that no one will believe his story, which leaves him only one option: to take down the DHS himself.

ABOUT THE AUTHOR: **Cory Doctorow** is a coeditor of *BoingBoing* and the former European director of the Electronic Frontier Foundation. He writes columns for *Make, Information Week*, the *Guardian* online, and *Locus*. He has won the *Locus* Award three times, been nominated for the Hugo and the Nebula, won the Campbell Award, and was named one of the Web's twenty-five influencers by *Forbes* magazine and a Young Global Leader by the World Economic Forum. He hopes you'll use technology to change the world.

1. How does Marcus's comment that he's "one of the most surveyed people in the world" set the tone for the novel? Is the statement true? Compare the school Marcus describes in the opening chapters to your own in terms of surveillance, discipline, and student-administrator relationships.

2. In what year or decade do you think *Little Brother* takes place? Cite passages from the novel to support your answer. Do you think the story could happen today? Why or why not?

3. Is Marcus a good kid or a bad kid? Can he be defined by either of those terms? How might Marcus describe his code of ethics regarding being "surveyed" and his right to circumvent the efforts of the survey-ors? How might you define the "moral dilemma" of reprogramming RFIDs, as explained in the novel?

4. What does Marcus's refusal to give passwords to and answer questions from government interrogators reveal about his character? How are passwords a recurring motif in the novel?

5. How does the author use Marcus's mother and father to represent different points of view about government oversight of individuals? Which parent best represents your perspective?

6. Does the media overemphasize identity theft and internet predators while underplaying the danger of being "watched" by legal government and corporate agencies through credit card use, transportation monitoring, etc.? How has this imbalance occurred and is surveillance the greater danger?

7. "Don't Trust Anyone Over 25" becomes an XNet motto and then a merchandized slogan. How does today's internet quicken public adoption of new ideas? Is this a good thing, a dangerous thing, or both?

8. How does Marcus's physical relationship with Ange affect his actions and attitudes? Is the absence of physical contact an important consideration when studying the internet? Do people treat others the same way in internet conversations as they do face-to-face? If not, what are the differences?

9. Is widely disseminated information always less lethal than a carefully kept secret (e.g., a how-to on weapons building or an encryption method)? Is this a great paradox of the information age?

10. Are government attempts to "protect" citizens through surveillance ridiculous to anyone with an understanding of security technology? Would America be safer if all of its citizens learned more about the computers upon which they rely? How else could/should America be made safe? By whom? From whom?

LIVE BOLDLY
Cultivate the Qualities That Can Change Your Life

AUTHOR: *Mary Anne Radmacher*

PUBLISHER: Conari Press, September 2008

WEBSITE: www.conari.com
www.maryanneradmacher.com

AVAILABLE IN:
Trade Paperback, 208 pages, $16.00
ISBN: 978-1-573-24321-6

SUBJECT: Identity/Personal Discovery/
Women's Lives (Nonfiction)

"This is an amazing book. The writing is so exquisitely beautiful, the ideas so wise, and the suggested applications so sensible, that reading it is like being a member of a celestial choir—you feel an essential part of something greater than yourself, something immediate, good and lasting." —**Hugh Prather, author of** *The Little Book of Letting Go* **and** *Morning Notes*

SUMMARY: In *Live Boldly*, Mary Anne Radmacher identifies an assortment of qualities for our life's journey and defines each as it relates to laughing loudly, loving truly, playing often, working smartly, and sharing your heart. Each definition is followed by a quote, a poem, an aphorism that explores the quality. Whether readers need or want justice or gratitude, endurance or celebration, comfort or challenge, the process is the same—read and listen to the word, enter into its meaning in the lives of others and bring that meaning to your own life.

ABOUT THE AUTHOR: **Mary Anne Radmacher** lives on Whidbey Island, Washington. For many years she lived in Salem, Oregon, where she ran a retail and wholesale business selling her art, posters, and cards. She continues that business. Radmacher also is a speaker and trainer for Participant Centered Results and does workshops on living a full, creative, balanced life. Her saying, "Courage does not always roar. Sometimes courage is the quiet voice at the end of the day saying, 'I will try again tomorrow,'" is cited in the *2006 Oxford Dictionary of American Quotations*. Her first book, *Lean Forward into Your Life*, was published by Conari Press in 2007.

1. "To live boldly is to create a synthesis between your observed and your unobserved life." What do you think that means? What does "to live boldly," mean to you?

2. Mary Anne suggests it's possible to cultivate qualities we don't naturally possess. Does our nature determine our qualities? Is it really possible to change our own lives?

3. "Everybody picks things to believe in. I believe I'll believe in this." Do you agree that people CHOOSE what they will believe in? Or do beliefs just sort of happen as a function of our parents and our community? What do you BELIEVE IN? What did you CHOOSE to believe in? What beliefs do you have that you didn't CONSCIOUSLY choose?

4. Ten consistent elements of a life lived boldly are listed in the afterword. What are ten consistent elements in your bold day?

5. The phrase "don't wait" is repeatedly used in the afterword. What is the significance of not waiting to which Mary Anne is referring? Isn't waiting part of being patient?

6. Mary Anne uses her life experiences to inspire others to cultivate the qualities that can change their lives. If you were to write a book from your own experience what would it be called and what would it be about?

7. Many events that Mary Anne shares could be classified as "failures," although she has a slightly different attitude toward failure than many folks do. How could that attitude have an impact on your day?

8. "The most significant elements in my days are laughter, learning, and applying my finest efforts to each endeavor." Do you identify with this? What would you say are the most significant elements of your days?

9. "Those who have entertained my life with their challenge and difficulty, those who see me through the lens of both adversary and adversity . . . I thank you for the profound lessons you have offered me in living my life boldly. While I will not name you, I most certainly will always remember you." Why does Mary Anne end her book expressing gratitude to her adversaries and adversities?

10. Is it really possible to live your life "as if no one were watching?" When? How might this change your experience today?

THE LOST MEMOIRS OF JANE AUSTEN

AUTHOR: *Syrie James*

PUBLISHER: Avon A, November 2007

WEBSITE: www.avonbooks.com
www.syriejames.com

AVAILABLE IN:
Trade Paperback, 337 pages, $13.95
ISBN: 978-0-06-134142-7

SUBJECT: Women's Lives/Social Issues/
History (Historical Fiction)

"Suspense builds, and it's a tribute to the world James creates that readers will anxiously root for Jane to find true love and wealth even though we know it never happened. Deserves front-runner status in the saturated field of Austen fan-fiction and film." —Kirkus Reviews

SUMMARY: What if, hidden in an old attic chest, Jane Austen's memoirs were discovered after hundreds of years? That's the premise behind this spellbinding novel, which delves into the secrets of Jane Austen's life, giving us untold insights into her mind and heart.

Jane Austen has given up her writing when, on a fateful trip to Lyme, she meets the well-read and charming Mr. Ashford, a man who is her equal in intellect and temperament. Inspired by the people and places around her, and encouraged by his faith in her, Jane begins revising *Sense and Sensibility*, a book she began years earlier, hoping to be published at last.

Deft and witty, written in a style that echoes Austen's own, this unforgettable novel offers a delightfully possible scenario for the inspiration behind this beloved author's romantic tales.

ABOUT THE AUTHOR: **Syrie James** is a scholar of 19th-century British literature and a long-time admirer of Jane Austen's work. A member of the Writer's Guild of America, Syrie is a screenwriter and playwright; this is her first work of historical fiction.

1. Why did the author choose to write the story in the first person, as Jane Austen's Memoirs? Do you think the novel would have been as effective if written in the third person narrative? Did you find yourself connecting with Jane Austen because it was written from her perspective?

2. Which character archetypes do we see in *The Lost Memoirs* that are reflections of the archetypes in Jane Austen's novels?

3. Discuss the ways in which Mr. Ashford is influential in rekindling Jane's interest in writing, and how the ups and downs of Jane's relationship with him are interwoven into the plot of her revised version of *Sense and Sensibility*.

4. In her unfinished novel, *The Watsons*, her heroine says: "Poverty is a great evil, but to a woman of education and feeling it ought not, it cannot be the greatest. I would rather be a teacher at a school (and I can think of nothing worse) than marry a man I did not like." Do you think this statement reveals Jane Austen's personal feelings? How is this theme expressed in The *Lost Memoirs*?

5. Discuss the pros and cons of *primogeniture*, which left all the land to the eldest son, and *entail*, which prevented the heir from dividing up the estate or selling any part of it. How did this enable the great landed families in 19th century England to maintain their wealth, status and power through the generations?

6. Cassandra, shortly before she died, went through Jane's letters, burning most of them and cutting out portions of others, before sharing them with her family. Why do you think Cassandra did this?

7. Were you surprised when you learned Mr. Ashford's secret? Discuss what might have happened if he'd been honest with Jane from the start. What does Jane's returning all of his letters unopened say about her? Do you consider it justifiable, or a character flaw?

8. While reading *The Lost Memoirs*, did you learn anything new or surprising about Jane Austen's life, and/or the customs or social conventions during Jane Austen's era?

9. What was your perception of Jane Austen and her work before you read *The Lost Memoirs*? Do you feel the same or differently after reading the novel?

10. What are some of your favorite moments in the book?

11. How did your experience reading *The Lost Memoirs* compare to Jane Austen novels you have read? In what ways was it similar or different? If you are not familiar with Jane Austen's work, did *The Lost Memoirs* inspire you to read her novels? Why or why not?

THE MEMORY KEEPER'S DAUGHTER

AUTHOR: *Kim Edwards*

PUBLISHER: Penguin Books, May 2006

WEBSITE: www.penguin.com

AVAILABLE IN:
Trade Paperback, 401 pages, $14.00
ISBN: 978-0-143-03714-9

SUBJECT: Relationships/Family/
Personal Challenges (Fiction)

"Kim Edwards writes with great wisdom and compassion. . . . This is a wonderful, heartbreaking, heart-healing novel." —**Luanne Rice**

"Anyone would be struck by the extraordinary power and sympathy of The Memory Keeper's Daughter.*"* —***The Washington Post***

"Kim Edwards has written a novel so mesmerizing that I devoured it." —***Sena Jeter Naslund***

"Edwards is a born novelist. . . . The Memory Keeper's Daughter *is rich with psychological detail and the nuances of human connection."* —***Chicago Tribune***

SUMMARY: This stunning novel begins on a winter night in 1964, when a blizzard forces Dr. David Henry to deliver his own twins. His son, born first, is perfectly healthy, but the doctor immediately recognizes that his daughter has Down's syndrome. For motives he tells himself are good, he makes a split-second decision that will haunt all their lives forever. He asks his nurse, Caroline, to take the baby away to an institution. Instead, she disappears into another city to raise the child as her own. Compulsively readable and deeply moving, *The Memory Keeper's Daughter* is a brilliantly crafted story of parallel lives, familial secrets, and the redemptive power of love.

ABOUT THE AUTHOR: **Kim Edwards** is the author of the short story collection *The Secrets of the Fire King*, which was an alternate for the 1998 PEN/Hemmingway Award, and she has won both the Whiting Award and the Nelson Algren Award. A graduate of the Iowa Writer's Workshop, she is an assistant professor of English at the University of Kentucky.

1. When David hands his baby girl over to Caroline and tells Norah that she has died, what was your immediate emotional reaction? At this early point, did you understand David's motivations? Did your understanding grow as the novel progressed?

2. Discuss David's psyche, his history, and what led him to make that fateful decision on the night of his children's birth.

3. When David instructs Caroline to take Phoebe to the institution, Caroline could have flatly refused or she could have gone to the authorities. Why doesn't she? Was she right to do what she did and raise Phoebe as her own? Was Caroline morally obligated to tell Norah the truth right from the beginning? Or was her moral obligation simply to take care of Phoebe at whatever cost? Why does she come to Norah after David's death?

4. Throughout the novel, the characters often describe themselves as feeling as if they are watching their own lives from the outside. For instance, David describes the moment when his wife is going into labor and says "he felt strangely as if he himself were suspended in the room . . . watching them both from above." What do you think Edwards is trying to convey here? Have you ever experienced similar feelings in your own life?

5. After Norah has successfully destroyed the wasps' nest, Edwards writes that there was something happening in Norah's life, "an explosion, some way in which life could never be the same." What does she mean, and what is the significance of Norah's "fight" with these wasps?

6. When David meets Rosemary it turns out to be a cathartic experience for him. What is it about her that enables David to finally speak the truth? Why does he feel compelled to take care of her?

7. The secret that David keeps is enormous and ultimately terribly destructive to himself and his family. Can you imagine a circumstance when it might be the right choice to shield those closest to you from the truth?

8. What do you think Norah's reaction would have been if David had been honest with her from the beginning? How might Norah have responded to the news that she had a daughter with Down's Syndrome? How might each of their lives have been different if David had not handed Phoebe to Caroline that fateful day?

THE MIDDLE PLACE

AUTHOR: *Kelly Corrigan*

PUBLISHER: Voice, January 2008

WEBSITE: www.everywomansvoice.com
www.kellycorrigan.com

AVAILABLE IN:
Hardcover, 272 pages, $23.95
ISBN: 978-1-4013-0336-5

SUBJECT: Women's Lives/
Coming of Age/Family (Memoir)

"The Middle Place *is a memoir that reads like a novel and sings like an Irish tenor. When Kelly Corrigan writes, she makes you want to come home."* —**Jacquelyn Mitchard, author of** *The Deep End of the Ocean* **and** *Still Summer*

"The Middle Place *is inspiring, luminous, and true. Reading this memoir, I felt like an honorary member of the Corrigan family . . . Kelly Corrigan is a wonderful writer."* —**Luanne Rice, author of** *What Matters Most*

SUMMARY: For Kelly Corrigan, family is everything. At thirty-six, she had a marriage that worked, a couple of funny, active kids, and a weekly newspaper column. But even as a thriving adult, Kelly still saw herself as George Corrigan's daughter. Kelly lives deep within what she calls the Middle Place—"that sliver of time when parenthood and childhood overlap"—comfortably wedged between her adult duties and her parents' care. But she's abruptly shoved into a coming-of-age when she finds a lump in her breast—and gets the diagnosis no one wants to hear.

ABOUT THE AUTHOR: **Kelly Corrigan** is, more than anything else, the mother of two young girls. While they're at school, Kelly writes a newspaper column, the occasional magazine article, and possible chapters of a novel. She is also the creator of CircusOfCancer.org, a website to teach people how to help a friend through breast cancer. Kelly lives outside San Francisco with her husband, Edward Lichty.

1. What is the effect of having the book structured as it is? Why do you think Kelly's childhood is presented as flashbacks rather than chronologically? In what ways does her childhood affect her adult self?

2. What role does religion play in the Corrigan family? How do you think Kelly feels about her parents' faith? About her own? What sorts of things does Kelly believe in?

3. How do you think Kelly feels about her mother? What does she seem to want from her and what does she actually get from her? What events cause her to see her mother differently over time?

4. How do Kelly's parents help her to feel secure and protected as a child? How does that continue or fade in her adult life? Which of her parents does she emulate in her own role as a parent?

5. How does Kelly's breast cancer diagnosis prepare her for her father's cancer? Does her own experience help her to help her father, or does it hinder her ability to cope?

6. Given her attachment to her family, why do you think Kelly moves so far away from home at the age of twenty-five? Do you think families need to live physically close to one another to remain emotionally close? Why or why not?

7. Kelly plays the role of both patient and caretaker. How does being a patient change her? How does being a caretaker change her? Do you think having an illness matures Kelly? Does caring for her father?

8. Why do you think it is important for Kelly to travel in Australia and Nepal? What need does the act of traveling fill for her?

9. How does Kelly change when she becomes a parent? In what ways does she choose the family she's created over the one that created her? Do you think is a common occurrence as we mature into adulthood?

10. Do people need crisis—like the illness or death of a parent—to become full-fledged adults? Is it possible to outgrow childhood without losing a parent? In what ways do our parents keep us in the "child" role?

11. How does Kelly learn to be sick? How much help do you think she should have accepted from others, and how much should she explain and share with those trying to help? What are the benefits she finds from letting people be involved? How do Kelly's attitudes about sickness differ from her father's?

12. What is "The Middle Place"? Why is this the title of this book? What does being in *The Middle Place* mean to Kelly? What does it mean to you?

THE MONSTERS OF TEMPLETON

AUTHOR: *Lauren Groff*

PUBLISHER: Voice, November 2008

WEBSITE: www.everywomansvoice.com
www.themonstersoftempleton.com

AVAILABLE IN:
Trade Paperback, 384 pages, $14.95
ISBN: 978-1-4013-4092-6

SUBJECT: Family/Personal Discovery/
Mystery (Fiction)

"There are monsters, murders, bastards, and ne'er-do-wells almost without number. I was sorry to see this rich and wonderful novel come to an end, and there is no higher success than that." —**Stephen King**

SUMMARY: In the wake of a wildly disastrous affair with her married archaeology professor, Willie Upton arrives on the doorstep of her ancestral home in Templeton, New York, where her hippie-turned-born-again-Baptist mom, Vi, still lives. Willie expects to be able to hide in the place that has been home to her family for generations, but the monster's death changes the fabric of the quiet, picture-perfect town her ancestors founded. Even further, Willie learns that the story her mother had always told her about her father has all been a lie: he wasn't the random man from a free-love commune that Vi had led her to imagine, but someone else entirely. Someone from this very town. As Willie puts her archaeological skills to work digging for the truth about her lineage, she discovers that the secrets of her family run deep. Through letters, editorials, and journal entries, the dead rise up to tell their sides of the story as dark mysteries come to light, past and present blur, old stories are finally put to rest, and the shocking truth about more than one monster is revealed.

ABOUT THE AUTHOR: **Lauren Groff** was born in Cooperstown, New York, which is the model for Templeton, her novel's setting. Her second book, *Delicate Edible Birds*, is a collection of short stories, some of which were previously published in *The Atlantic Monthly*, *Ploughshares*, *The Best American Short Stories*, and *Pushcart Prize* anthologies. She lives in Gainesville, Florida.

1. What did you think of the range of voices and time periods the author employs in *The Monsters of Templeton*? How would the novel have been different had the story been told from a single point of view, or been set in one era?

2. Why are so many people in Templeton affected by the monster's death? What did the monster represent to them?

3. Given her conflicted relationship with her mother and, to a lesser extent, with her hometown, why do you think Willie Upton decides to go back to Templeton? What was Willie looking for when she returned to Templeton? Does she find it?

4. In what instances do ghosts make appearances in *The Monsters of Templeton*? What do the ghosts represent? What other symbols does the author employ in the novel? What do they mean?

5. For twenty-eight years, Vivienne has told her daughter that Willie was the product of a hippie commune. The day that Willie returns home, she decides to tell her the truth: that her father was a man in Templeton. What would you have done if you were in Willie's position? Or in Vivienne's?

6. Of the many characters from the past—Marmaduke Temple, Davey Shipman, Charlotte and Cinnamon, Elizabeth Franklin Temple, to name a few—which one(s) stood out for you? Why?

7. What did you think of Willie's search to uncover her father's identity? What did each new layer of history teach Willie about her family? Why was it important that Willie learn everything she learned?

8. What was your opinion of Ezekiel Felcher at the beginning of the novel? Did it change as the novel progressed? Did you think that Willie might stay in Templeton to be with him? What do you think she should have done? What do you think she will do in the future?

9. "This is a story of creation," says Marmaduke Temple in one of the epigrams before the book begins, ostensibly an excerpt from his own story about how he founded Templeton. In what other ways is *The Monsters of Templeton* a story of creation? How can Willie's story been seen as a story of creation?

10. *The Monsters of Templeton* ends with a death and a birth. What does this mean in the larger context of the novel? Who—or what—else is born in the book?

11. What does the book's title mean? Who or what are the "monsters" it refers to? What, exactly, does the word "monster" mean in the context of this book?

MY HANDS CAME AWAY RED

AUTHOR: *Lisa McKay*

PUBLISHER: Moody Publishers
September 2007

WEBSITE: www.lisamckaywriting.com
AVAILABLE IN:
Trade Paperback, 391 pages, $12.99
ISBN: 978-0-8024-8982-1

SUBJECT: Faith/Culture & World Issues/
Personal Discovery (Fiction)

"In this fast-paced, thought-provoking debut novel, McKay . . . explores injustice, religious reconciliation, suffering and faith . . . one of Christian fiction's best novels of the year." —Publishers Weekly

SUMMARY: Thinking largely of escaping a complicated love-life and having fun on the beach, eighteen-year old Cori signs up for a ten-week trip to help build a church on a remote island in Indonesia.

Six weeks into the trip, a conflict that has been simmering for years flames to deadly life on the nearby island of Ambon. Before they can leave, Cori and her teammates find themselves caught up in the destructive wave of violence washing over the Christian and Muslim villages in the area. Within days, they are forced to flee into the hazardous refuge of the mountains with only the pastor's son to guide them.

As the team hikes through the jungle, Cori's search for spiritual answers and emotional stability proves just as difficult as the physical journey home.

Background Note: While the characters in this story are fictional, they experienced a real-world conflict. Events very similar to those depicted in this story have occurred in the Maluku Islands of Indonesia within the last decade.

ABOUT THE AUTHOR: **Lisa McKay** is an Australian forensic psychologist. She is currently living in Los Angeles and working as the Director of Training and Education Services for the Headington Institute, which provides psychological and spiritual support services to humanitarian workers worldwide.

1. To what extent do the characters of this book remind you of yourself or someone you know?

2. What scene(s) did you find had the most emotional impact? Why?

3. Did any part of the story make you uncomfortable or angry? If so, why?

4. What themes and/or questions stood out to you as you read this book? How did different characters in the story interact with these themes?

5. How do the various characters react to the massacre in Mani's village and the events that followed? Did you learn anything about the experience of trauma through their stories? Which character did you identify with most?

6. Marooned in the jungle, what was Cori thinking and feeling as she read Psalm 55? Have you experienced events in your life that could have prompted similar questions and feelings? How did you react in those times? How do you address such questions in your own life, now?

7. How did Cori react after returning home? Why might she have reacted like that? Were you surprised by any of her reactions? How were they similar or different to experiences you or others have had after returning from spending time overseas?

8. How have the various characters changed by the end of the novel? What changes were "positive/negative"? Why?

9. Has reading this book prompted you to reconsider some of your views or investigate further some of the issues raised (e.g. faith-based or sectarian conflicts, post-traumatic stress)?

10. Do you think "my hands came away red" is a good title for the book? Why or why not? What are some of the images and meanings the title evokes?

11. Where did you see laughter, joy, and hope in this story? Where did the characters find them? When things seem darkest in your own life where do you tend to find those things?

12. Throughout the novel, the characters frequently make up their own stories about a boy named Jip and his pet monkey, Kiki. What did Jip and Kiki come to mean to the characters in the story? What role(s) did they play as a literary device?

13. What can you do to better understand people who have a different faith or worldview?

THE NIGHT CLIMBERS

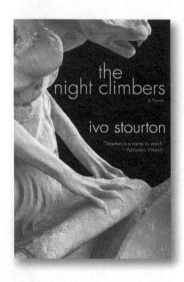

AUTHOR: *Ivo Stourton*

PUBLISHER Simon Spotlight Entertainment
June 2008

WEBSITE: www.simonsays.com

AVAILABLE IN:
Trade Paperback, 336 pages, $14.00
ISBN: 978-1-4165-8841-2

SUBJECT: History/Adventure/Identity
(Fiction)

"An amazingly accomplished debut. . . . The writing is elegant, the story decadent." —**Observer**

"Loved The Line of Beauty, *mooned over* Brideshead, *lapped up* The Secret History? *Then this one's for you. . . . Stourton really can write."* —**Independent on Sunday**

SUMMARY: When James Walker arrives at Tudor College, Cambridge, he tries to create a vague air of mystery about himself in the hope of making the right kind of friends. By accident or fate he encounters a member of the Night Climbers, a wealthy, secretive, and tantalizingly eccentric circle of undergraduates who scale the college towers and gargoyles at night in pursuit of the kind of thrill-seeking danger that makes them feel truly alive. Seduced by their reckless charisma and talent for decadence, James falls for both Francis, the group's ringleader, and Jessica, his beautiful best friend. Their extravagant living is financed, unwittingly, by Francis's father, but when he suddenly cuts his son off, the friends are left floundering as they try to maintain a lifestyle they can't afford. That is, until Francis embroils them in a plan that will test the limits of their friendship and link them to one another forever. Humming with intellectual energy and grace, *The Night Climbers* portrays the intensity of early relationships, when people are at their most impressionable, and explores the ties that bind with a keen eye.

ABOUT THE AUTHOR: **Ivo Stourton** was born in 1982 and received high honors in English at Cambridge. This is his first novel.

1. How did your opinion of the characters shift throughout the novel, especially your attitude toward James and Francis? Which of your initial assumptions proved to be false?
2. What drew Michael to James? Was James inducted into the Night Climbers because he created the illusion that he fit the criteria, or because Michael knew that he really wasn't like the other members?
3. Discuss the novel's title. Besides their literal climbing, what other daring heights did the group aspire to reach? What might have compelled the campus's real-life climbers throughout history to perform their legendary expeditions? Is it simply a reflection of a quest for an adrenaline rush, or does it mean something more?
4. What led Francis to become highly addicted, while James managed to avoid a similar spiral? Was Francis's urge to test the limits of the body related to his fascination with cadavers, illustrated in chapter seven?
5. What is the role of illusion and storytelling within the circle of Night Climbers? Does good storytelling trump truthful storytelling in the real world?
6. What does sex mean to James, Jessica, and Frances? What levels of intimacy—emotional and physical—are they able to experience? Do they view sex only as a rush, or as a way to bond?
7. What finally compels Lord Soulford's decision to disinherit his son in chapter twelve? What is your understanding of their relationship? How is Francis's experience of family different from James's?
8. In terms of personality, what was Lisa's role in the group? What made her an essential player in pulling off the Picasso sale? What were her best survival traits?
9. What does money mean to each of the characters? What accounts for Francis's voracious appetite for spending, versus Lisa's incredibly good investing skills?
10. How did you react to the structure of the novel, featuring shifting timelines? Does it reflect your own experience of memory, and the way past events often mingle with the present?
11. Did you agree with Francis's philosophy that creating a fake is not immoral if society cannot tell the difference between a fake and an original, attaching perceived value to unseen attributes?
12. Could anyone or anything have saved Francis from the level of despair that ended his life?
13. How would you describe James's tone as a narrator? How might the novel have unfolded if it had been told from Francis's point of view?

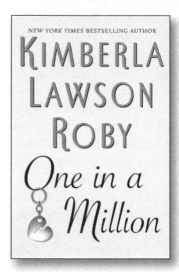

NEW YORK TIMES BESTSELLING AUTHOR

KIMBERLA LAWSON ROBY

One in a Million

ONE IN A MILLION

AUTHOR: *Kimberla Lawson Roby*

PUBLISHER: William Morrow, June 2008

WEBSITE: www.williammorrow.com
www.kimroby.com

AVAILABLE IN:
Hardcover, 192 pages, $19.95
ISBN: 978-0-06-144295-7

SUBJECT: Relationships/Personal
Challenges/Women's Lives (Fiction)

SUMMARY: Kennedi Mason thinks she's the luckiest woman on earth. She loves her job, she has a wonderful best friend, and she's been married for ten years to her soul mate. There's nothing she can think of that could make her life any better.

Then one fateful day Kennedi receives a piece of news that will turn her world upside down. She's excited about it, and she knows that her husband, Blake, will be over the moon. He has always dreamed of this one thing happening, and she can't wait until he comes home so she can tell him.

But when she sees Blake that evening, he has a special announcement of his own. It shocks Kennedi into silence and wipes the admission she was planning to make right out of her mind. In an instant, her life and her marriage have changed, but not at all in the way that she had expected.

A poignant and satisfying story of hope, Kimberla Lawson Roby's *One in a Million* beautifully shows us the difference between what we think we want and what we actually need to be truly happy.

ABOUT THE AUTHOR: **Kimberla Lawson Roby** is the author of the acclaimed novels *Sin No More, Love and Lies, Changing Faces, The Best-Kept Secret, Too Much of a Good Thing, A Taste of Reality, Behind Closed Doors, Here and Now, Casting the First Stone,* and *It's a Thin Line.* She lives with her husband in Illinois.

1. Before reading the last few lines of the first chapter, what did you think Kennedi's surprise news was going to be? What type of news did you think Blake had for her?

2. Have you ever been told by a husband or boyfriend that he was cheating on you and if so, in what ways did you react to the situation? How do you think a person should respond when this happens—end the relationship or forgive and move on?

3. When Kennedi and Patrice see Blake and Serena at the restaurant having lunch, were you satisfied with the way she confronted them? Why or why not? How would you have handled the situation?

4. After a short time passes, Kennedi realizes that Blake may not have used protection and that she has no choice but to get an H.I.V. test. Do you believe the rate of unprotected sex will ever decrease? If not, why do you think people continue to be so careless?

5. Do you think Kennedi contributed to Blake's philandering, and if so, how? In a situation like this, do you think the fault is that of one person alone or do you believe there are always two sides to every story?

6. What is the first thing you would do if you won millions of dollars? Would you share it with relatives and/or friends? What are some of the fun things you would do to enjoy yourself?

7. At this very moment, are you blessed enough to have a best friend like Patrice, one who will stand by you during both good and not so happy times? How much of your lottery winnings would you give her or him?

8. Matthew 19:24 says "And again I say unto you, it is easier for a camel to go through the eye of a needle, than for a rich man to enter into the kingdom of God." So, do you believe Kennedi and her accountant fall into this category (even though they tithe at their churches and help those who are less fortunate than they are) or do you believe being wealthy is fine as long as you are constantly helping others? Why?

9. Did you feel that Blake was entitled to any of the winnings whatsoever? If so, please explain why?

10. Did you like Miles from the very beginning or did you suspect he had ulterior motives? If so, what did you think those motives might be?

11. Were you shocked to find out who was betraying Kennedi's trust? Have you ever had family members, friends, or acquaintances betray you in a very painful way, specifically because of greed?

12. Were you happy that Blake's whole blackmail scheme basically blew up in his face? Were you satisfied with the way things turned out for Kennedi?

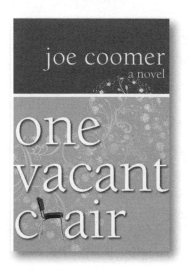

ONE VACANT CHAIR

AUTHOR: *Joe Coomer*

PUBLISHER: Graywolf Press
          September 2008

WEBSITE: www.graywolfpress.org

AVAILABLE IN:
Trade Paperback, 288 pages, $14.00
ISBN: 978-1-55597-514-2

SUBJECTS: Family/Relationships/Identity
(Fiction)

"An enjoyable read, without a dull page." —*Kirkus Reviews*

SUMMARY: At the funeral of Grandma Hutton—whom Edna has cared for through an agonizingly long and vague illness—Sarah begins helping her aunt clean up the last of a life. This includes honoring Grandma's wish to have her ashes scattered in Scotland—although she had never left the state of Texas.

"We were two fat women, eighteen years apart, a chair artist and a designer of Christmas ornaments, who only knew we had troubles and a hot summer to get through," says Sarah. But as it turns out, there is a great deal more to her quirky aunt's troubles than Sarah could possibly imagine. As the novel turns from the oppressive heat of Texas to the cool, misty beauty of Scotland, she learns of her Aunt Edna's remarkable secret life and comes to fully understand the fragile business of living and even dying.

ABOUT THE AUTHOR: **Joe Coomer** is the much celebrated author of *Beachcombing for a Shipwrecked God*, *A Flatland Fable*, and *The Loop*, which was a *New York Times* Book of the Year. He splits his time between Texas and Maine.

1. In the opening chapter, the revelation of Sam's affair radically shifts the way Sarah views her husband, their marriage, and her plans for the future. After traveling to Scotland with Aunt Edna, have Sarah's feelings concerning the affair changed? Will she leave Sam, or will they work through their marital problems?

2. Sarah says she loves Aunt Edna and regrets not seeing her sooner. What do you make of Sarah's decision to stay with Edna? Is it motivated by love? Is it an act of revenge? A form of self-protection? Avoidance?

3. Sarah's parents, Aunt Edna, and James all provide Sarah with advice about her marriage. All three seem to suggest that Sarah should give Sam another chance, or at least give him an opportunity to explain his actions. What do you think about their opinions? Does Sarah take them to heart?

4. In Plockton, Aunt Edna puts her fingers in her mouth and sucks them clean of her mother's remaining ashes after she scatters them. What do you make of this action? What does it mean?

5. What do you think Aunt Edna is trying to say when she compares Bean Highe, the washerwoman, to Sarah?

6. Did your opinion of Aunt Edna change after she revealed how her mother died? Why or why not?

7. When Sarah goes to Jonathan's house to talk about Aunt Edna, her cancer, and the future of all her paintings, she asks Jonathan to draw her. Why? Does she have anything to feel ashamed about?

8. Do you agree with Aunt Edna's belief that it was right to hide her pancreatic cancer and the true nature of her mother's death from James until after their wedding?

9. Do you think Sarah's actions were justified when she did what Aunt Edna asked? What do you think motivated her decision to follow Aunt Edna's instructions?

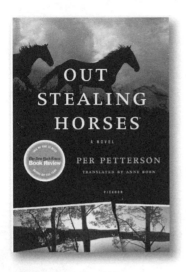

OUT STEALING HORSES

AUTHOR: *Per Petterson*

PUBLISHER: Picador, May 2008

WEBSITE: www.picadorusa.com

AVAILABLE IN:
Trade Paperback, 256 pages, $14.00
ISBN: 978-0-312-42708-5

SUBJECT: Personal Discovery/
Family/Relationships (Fiction)

"A gripping account of such originality as to expand the reader's own experience of life." —**Thomas McGuane, *The New York Times Book Review***

"Read Out Stealing Horses *by Per Petterson. From the first terse sentences of this mesmerizing Norwegian novel about youth, memory, and, yes, horse stealing, you know you're in the hands of a master storyteller."* —***Newsweek***

"That's the effect of Per Petterson's award-winning novel: It hits you in the heart at close range." —**Alan Cheuse, NPR's *All Things Considered***

"Petterson's spare and deliberate prose has astonishing force. . . . Loss is conveyed with all the intensity of a boy's perception but acquires new resonance in the brooding consciousness of the older man." —***The New Yorker***

SUMMARY: *Out Stealing Horses* has been embraced across the world as a classic, a novel of universal relevance and power. Panoramic and gripping, it tells the story of Trond Sander, a sixty-seven-year-old man who has moved from the city to a remote, riverside cabin, only to have all the turbulence, grief, and overwhelming beauty of his youth come back to him one night while he's out on a walk. From the moment Trond sees a strange figure coming out of the dark behind his home, the reader is immersed in a decades-deep story of searching and loss, and in the precise, irresistible prose of a newly crowned master of fiction.

ABOUT THE AUTHOR: **Per Petterson** was a librarian and a bookseller before becoming a novelist. He lives in Oslo, Norway.

1. Do you think Trond is happy in his isolation? Is he making a brave choice by withdrawing to the country, as he has always dreamt of doing; or do you think he's fleeing the responsibilities of his life?

2. Soon after Odd is killed, Trond says "I felt it somewhere inside me; a small remnant, a bright yellow speck that perhaps would never leave me." What is it he feels? How does that day stealing horses with Jon, and learning what has happened to Odd, change Trond? Do you see the effects of that loss in him as an older man?

3. After his dream at the start of Chapter 5, which leaves him weeping, Trond says, "But then it is not death I fear." Do you believe him? If so, what is he afraid of?

4. How do you think Trond's life would have changed if he had hit the man in Karlstad? Why does he attach so much significance to that decision?

5. Look at the scene in which Trond's car goes off the road and he sees the lynx in the woods. Why does a near accident, and the sight of the lynx, thrill him?

6. Were you surprised by Ellen's reaction to her father when she finds him at the end of the book? Would you be angrier in her position, or more forgiving? Has Trond been unfair to her?

7. How has Trond become like his father, and how has he managed to take a different path? What parallels do you see between the lives they lead in the book? How is Trond's behavior as an adult influenced by the short time he spent with his father as a young man?

8. Look at the book's final section, after Trond has discovered that his father isn't coming back. How does his behavior change? Were you surprised by his reaction to the news?

9. Look at Ellen's monologue about the opening lines of *David Copperfield*. How do you understand the phenomenon she's describing, of not being "the leading characters of our own lives"? Has this happened to anyone you know? Do you think it has happened to Trond? Is it a good or a bad thing?

10. Why do you think Trond's father doesn't tell him the story of the Resistance? Why does he leave it to Franz? How do you think Trond's perception of his father would have changed if his father had told the story himself?

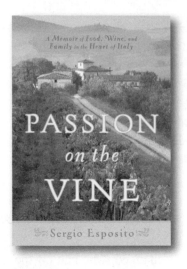

PASSION ON THE VINE
A Memoir of Food, Wine, and Family in the Heart of Italy

AUTHOR: *Sergio Esposito*

PUBLISHER: Broadway Books, April 2008

WEBSITE: www.broadwaybooks.com
www.passiononthevine.com

AVAILABLE IN:
Hardcover, 304 pages, $24.95
ISBN: 978-0-7679-2607-2

SUBJECT: History/Regional/Identity
(Memoir)

"Passion on the Vine *is a spellbinding memoir; a vivid, funny, and, yes, passionate tale of family, food, and wine. The tour de force chapter on his childhood in Naples will make you wish you were Italian. Sergio Esposito is not only a great epicurean—he's also a great storyteller. If he ever gets tired of selling wine, he's got a bright future as a writer."*
—**Jay McInerney**

"Esposito's glass is always half-full, when not filled to the brim, and always with something beautifully red and swirling and passionate, as are his words in this wine-adventure, story-memoir. His words are like the vines he so ardently writes about—earthy, deep-rooted; and the wines— perfect on the tongue, with a long finish." —**Frances Mayes**

SUMMARY: Infused with captivating images of a Neapolitan boyhood and a career devoted to the incomparable wonders of Italian wine, *Passion on the Vine* is an enchanting love letter to a singular destination, written not by an outsider but by one of its most devoted sons. Esposito has produced a unique book that defies categorization. A tender family saga, an inspiring tale of immigrant success, a captivating armchair-travel experience that whisks you to locales that even most Italians are barred from entering, this intoxicating memoir yields much for your reading group to savor.

ABOUT THE AUTHOR: **Sergio Esposito** is the owner of Italian Wine Merchants in New York City. He speaks at and hosts wine dinners throughout the country, has a much-visited Web site, and writes a popular e-mail newsletter about his discoveries and travels in Italy. He lives with his wife and two children in New York City.

1. What does it take to develop a passion for a life's work, or for an indulgence? What sparked Esposito's passion for wine?

2. What did the opening scenes help you discover about the realities of the wine trade? In what way do Esposito's direct, sometimes gritty depictions only enhance the experience of his writing?

3. How would you characterize the dynamics of Esposito's family? How was he influenced by his family stories of war and of a fallen aristocracy?

4. In the first chapter, Esposito describes his disappointment in discovering that a local restaurant no longer served traditional, regional cuisine. How has the power of critics grown in other fields as well? Is there a disconnect between the food and wine that critics praise and the choices that personally please you?

5. Esposito describes the mournful scene of his family's departure for America at the end of chapter two. What were the costs and benefits of the Espositos' departure from Naples?

6. What role does wine play in Italian culture? What does the author mean when he writes that "Italian wine, like Italian food, is simultaneously no big deal and the biggest possible deal"? Are American attitudes and laws regarding alcohol unhealthy?

7. What common denominator seems to exist among all of the legendary wineries Esposito reveres?

8. What did Josko Gravner's experience with cutting-edge technology say about the current schism between purists who see wine as a natural process and those who scorn ancient methods? Which would you prefer if you were to try to enter this business?

9. What cultural differences did you detect when Esposito and his wife crossed the border to call on Slovenian winemaker Ales Kristancic? What is symbolic about his sediment-laden bottles of Puro?

10. Does Luca Maroni, the radical modernist featured in chapter nine, have a future? How would the world's perceptions of wine change if his algebraic formula and his argument against aging proved to be effective?

11. How did the winemakers Esposito depicts in *Passion on the Vine* respond to the need to market themselves? How is image both an asset and a hindrance to artisans?

12. What does the twenty-first century promise in terms of American attitudes toward Europe in general and Italian exports specifically?

13. How has your own experience of wine changed throughout your lifetime? What are the traits of your favorite wines? How has Esposito affected your approach to choosing and enjoying Italian selections?

THE PERFECT SUMMER
England 1911, Just Before the Storm

AUTHOR: *Juliet Nicolson*

PUBLISHER: Grove Press, May 2008

WEBSITE: www.grovepress.com

AVAILABLE IN:
Trade Paperback, 304 pages, $15.00
ISBN: 978-0-8021-4367-9

SUBJECTS: History/Social Issues/Personal Challenges (Nonfiction)

"A hugely interesting portrait of a society teetering on a precipice both nationally and internationally. . . . As page turning as a novel."
—**Joanna Trollope,** *The Guardian*

"Absorbing. . . . A deeply pleasurable read." *—Kirkus Reviews* **(starred)**

SUMMARY: Through the tight lens of four months, Juliet Nicolson's rich storytelling gifts rivet us with the sights, colors, and feelings of a bygone era. But perfection was not for all. Cracks in the social fabric were showing: The country was brought to a standstill by industrial strikes. Led by the charismatic Ben Tillett, the Southampton Dockers' Union paralyzed shipping in the south. Organizer Mary Macarthur inspired women from the "sweated industries" to take to the streets in protest of intolerable conditions. Home Secretary Winston Churchill, fearing that the country was on the verge of collapse, gave in to demands for wage increases. Temperatures rose steadily to more than 100 degrees; by August, deaths from heatstroke were too many for newspapers to report. Drawing on material from intimate and rarely seen sources and narrated through the eyes of a series of exceptional individuals—among them a debutante, a choirboy, a politician, a trade unionist, a butler, and the queen—*The Perfect Summer* is a vividly rendered glimpse of the twilight of the Edwardian era.

ABOUT THE AUTHOR: **Juliet Nicolson** is the granddaughter of Vita Sackville-West and Harold Nicolson, and the daughter of Nigel Nicolson. A journalist and writer, she lives in London and Sissinghurst, Kent.

1. What is the paradox in the title of Nicolson's book? "It was a summer when, as the Countess of Fingall put it, 'We danced on the edge of an abyss.'"

2. In a country with a reputation for being straight-laced, this book pulls the curtains apart for some delightful aberrant behavior. Talk about some of the high jinks, discovered and undiscovered.

3. Do you sense any nostalgia for those days of 1911, even with all the class rigidity and vast gap between rich and poor?

4. Are you surprised the United States plays such a minimal role in Nicolson's England of 1911?

5. Does *The Perfect Summer* give you the idea that events of years following might have gone another direction? What might have made a difference?

6. Can you think of other books, even historical novels, that use research and detail in ways Nicolson does?

7. Do you feel Nicolson provides enough information about the coming cataclysm in Europe?

8. How does the weather become a central character?

9. Do you emerge from this book with a clear idea of what it is to be English . . . at least in 1911? Is there still a coherent norm at the time of the book? Are there vestiges of this world today among the English you know or read about?

10. What do we learn about the royal family, especially in the transition from Edward VII to George V? Does Queen Mary come alive for you? What are we told about the Prince of Wales (later Edward VIII)? Are there intimations of 1936?

11. Is the Rudyard Kipling of the book the one you recognize from his writings? What is his reputation at the time?

12. What are some astonishing examples of the upper class use and abuse of servants? Are your Masterpiece Theater ideas of upstairs-downstairs lives confirmed?

13. How is it that new members of the House of Lords included the writers J. M. Barrie, Bernard Shaw, and Thomas Hardy?

14. What are the reforms of the National Insurance Act proposed by Lloyd George? Why is it so controversial?

15. What kind of person is Ben Tillett? How would you explain his influence? Do you find him a compelling figure?

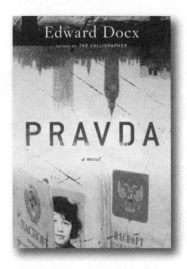

PRAVDA

AUTHOR: *Edward Docx*

PUBLISHER: Mariner Books, March 2008

WEBSITE: www.marinerbooks.com

AVAILABLE IN:
Trade Paperback, 400 pages $13.95
ISBN: 978-0-618-53440-1

SUBJECT: Family/Identity/Mystery
(Fiction)

**Long-listed for the 2007 Man Booker Prize
Winner of the Geoffrey Faber Memorial Prize**

"As in his previous book, the final twist is a stunner, both totally unexpected and carefully prepared for. . . . Well written, vigorously plotted and perceptive about human nature." —**Kirkus Reviews** (starred)

"Engrossing . . . Docx's story has a pleasing vitality, and the strands of it set in St Petersburg are particularly compelling. This is a solid novel." —**Daily Telegraph** UK

SUMMARY: Thirty-two-year-old Gabriel Glover arrives in St. Petersburg to find his mother dead in her apartment. Reeling from grief, Gabriel and his twin sister, Isabella, arrange the funeral without contacting their father, Nicholas, a brilliant and manipulative libertine. Unknown to the twins, their mother had long ago abandoned a son, Arkady, a pitiless Russian predator now determined to claim his birthright. Arkady sets out to find the siblings and uncover the dark secret hidden from them their entire lives. *Pravda* is a hauntingly beautiful chronicle of discovery and loss, love and loyalty, and the destructive legacy of deceit.

ABOUT THE AUTHOR: **Edward Docx** is the author of the acclaimed *The Calligrapher*, which was named a *San Francisco Chronicle* Best Book of the Year. He was a Sunday columnist and arts editor for national newspapers in the UK. Now a full-time writer, he still contributes to British and American newspapers and appears frequently as a cultural critic on television and radio.

1. The often quoted line from Shakespeare's *Romeo & Juliet*, "What's in a name? That which we call a rose / By any other name would smell as sweet," might seem emblematic of many of the themes of identity in *Pravda*. For example, when Nicholas remembers his wife as "Maria, Masha, Mashka, Marushya," is he thinking of someone whose true identity surpassed definition, or someone who was a composite of many names, many cultures?

2. What do you think of Nicholas's conception of love and attraction, and fidelity? (Do you think his ballet metaphor is helpful in understanding love?) Would you agree that there are different kinds of love, and that Nicholas had attained a kind of enlightenment by not repressing his conflicting (or complementary) attachments?

3. Do you think Gabriel believes himself to be like his father or his grandfather? Do you think he confronts his own infidelities because of them, or despite their influence?

4. Although their lives are superficially different, Henry and Gabriel are each struggling to attain a kind of purity of the soul. (And of the body, perhaps.) Does each succeed? What do you think of Henry's final actions?

5. Part Three begins with an epigraph, the famous lines from Marx "All that is solid melts into air, all that is holy is profaned . . ." How do these lines underscore the futility of our modern era, as experienced by Gabriel in his work with *Self Help?* How do they describe the familial quest at the heart of the novel? Why do you think the author chose this particular quote?

6. At the end of the novel, why do you think Isabella chooses to sponsor Arkady regardless of her assessment of his talent? Do you agree with her decision?

7. Do you think Arkady's lifelong illegitimacy is vindicated, at the end of the novel, by his piano skills? Or does the novel discourage a straightforward sense of identity, legitimacy, or entitlement in each of Maria's children?

8. Arkady is presented as a crude and scornful character, and yet he seems cognizant of his mother's emotional detachment in their only meeting. How would you have handled such a reunion?

9. Are Isabella and Gabriel forced to become more mature adults when confronting the lives of their parents?

10. How are the titles of the novel's periodicals emblematic of its main themes? What title would you have given the novel?

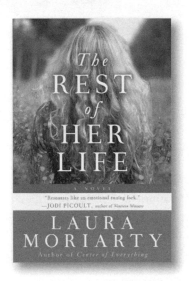

THE REST OF HER LIFE

AUTHOR: *Laura Moriarty*

PUBLISHER: Hyperion Books, June 2008

WEBSITE: www.lauramoriarty.net
www.hyperionbooks.com

AVAILABLE IN:
Trade Paperback, 352 pages, $14.95
ISBN: 978-1-4013-0943-5

SUBJECT: Family/Relationships/
Women's Lives (Fiction)

#1 August 2007 Book Sense Pick

"Are the sins of the parents visited upon the children, or vice versa? Laura Moriarty's raw, honest novel about an ordinary family whose life changes in one extraordinary moment resonates like an emotional tuning fork. You'll be asking yourself what you would do in this situation, long after you've finished reading." —**Jodi Picoult,** *New York Times* **bestselling author of** *My Sister's Keeper* **and** *Nineteen Minutes*

SUMMARY: In *The Rest of Her Life*, Laura Moriarty delivers a luminous, compassionate, and provocative look at how mothers and daughters with the best intentions can be blind to the harm they do to one another.

Leigh is the mother of high-achieving, popular high school senior Kara. Their relationship is already strained for reasons Leigh does not fully understand when, in a moment of carelessness, Kara makes a mistake that ends in tragedy the effects of which not only divide Leigh's family, but polarize the entire community.

Like the best works of Jane Hamilton, Jodi Picoult, and Alice Sebold, Laura Moriarty's *The Rest of Her Life* is a novel of complex moral dilemma, filled with nuanced characters and a page-turning plot that makes readers ask themselves, "What would I do?"

ABOUT THE AUTHOR: **Laura Moriarty** received her master's degree from the University of Kansas, and was awarded the George Bennett Fellowship for Creative Writing at Phillips Exeter Academy. Her first novel was *The Center of Everything*. She lives in Lawrence, Kansas.

1. Leigh is certainly a flawed human being. But what are her strengths—as a mother and as a human being? What are her weaknesses? If her weaknesses are a product of her difficult childhood, why is her sister so different?

2. In the course of the novel, the relationship between Leigh and Kara changes. What do you think of as the major turning point in their relationship? What do you think was at the heart of the conflict?

3. How important is the setting to this story? Would the same situation have played out differently in a larger town, a suburb, or a city? What do you think would have been the same?

4. At the beginning of the novel, Leigh believes she likes living in a small town like Danby because she likes the sense of community it offers. Is she really a part of this community? How does Leigh's relationship to the town change over the summer?

5. When Leigh accuses Eva of being a gossip, Eva defends herself by saying she just cares about what's happening in the lives of people in her community. Do you buy this? Leigh spends a lot of time worrying about what people are saying about her family, but is gossip ever a positive force in the story? Do you like Eva? Why or why not?

6. After hearing Eva deny being a gossip, Leigh is stunned: "People didn't see themselves, she considered. It was almost eerie when you saw it face to face." Who else in the novel might not see herself or himself clearly? Does anyone? Do you think of this selective "vision" as a conscious choice or a true inability?

7. Is Gary a better parent than Leigh? In what ways does his relationship with Justin mirror Leigh's relationship with Kara? What is it about each child that brings out such different responses from both Gary and Leigh?

8. The first time the bereaved mother confronts Kara, it is Leigh—not Gary—who steps in to protect her. Leigh believes she recognizes something in Diane Kletchka, something we can assume Gary does not. What do you think it is about Diane that feels familiar to Leigh?

9. In this novel, we see Leigh in several different kinds of relationships: she's a mother, a daughter, a sister, a wife, and a friend. How do all these different roles compete with each other for Leigh's attention/loyalty? Does she give too much attention to any one role? Not enough to another? In what ways do these different kinds of relationships influence one another?

RUN

AUTHOR: *Ann Patchett*

PUBLISHER: Harper Perennial
September 2008

WEBSITE: www.annpatchett.com
www.harperperennial.com

AVAILABLE IN:
Trade Paperback, 320 pages, $14.95
ISBN: 978-0-06-134064-2

SUBJECT: Family/Relationships/
Social Issues (Fiction)

"Patchett has once again written an intelligent, thoughtful novel that oozes emotional intensity. She is the kind of storyteller who makes the reader sad to come to the last page." —Financial Times

"Run is a book that sets out inventively to contend with the temper of our times, and by the end we feel we really know the Doyle family in all its intensity and with all its surprises." —Publishers Weekly

"Run is strongly recommended." —New York magazine

"Ms. Patchett comes home." —Wall Street Journal

SUMMARY: Since their mother's death, Tip and Teddy Doyle have been raised by their loving, possessive, and ambitious father. As the former mayor of Boston, Bernard Doyle wants to see his sons in politics, a dream the boys have never shared. But when an argument in a blinding New England snowstorm inadvertently causes an accident that involves a stranger and her child, all Bernard cares about is his ability to keep his children—all his children—safe.

ABOUT THE AUTHOR: **Ann Patchett** is the author of five novels, including *Bel Canto* (winner of the PEN/Faulkner Award and the Orange Prize), and the bestselling nonfiction book, *Truth & Beauty*. She has written for *The Atlantic, Harper's, Gourmet*, the *New York Times Magazine, Vogue*, and the *Washington Post*. She lives in Nashville, Tennessee.

1. How would you characterize Teddy and Tip's relationship as siblings? How does it compare to their relationship with their brother, Sullivan?
2. At the Jesse Jackson lecture, Doyle reviews the personalities of his three sons and thinks about which of them would be most able to lead. Which of the boys do you think would make the best politician? Do you think Doyle's assessments of their characters are accurate or biased?
3. Discuss the concept of nature versus nurture. Do you think that Sullivan, Tip, and Teddy would have turned out differently if Bernadette lived? How would those differences manifest themselves?
4. Discuss the different meanings of the title. How many different ways does the word "run" work for you?
5. *Run* includes several incidences of doubling—two brothers who get adopted, two mothers who die, two men named Sullivan, two Tennessee Alice Mosers, two accidents involving hospital stays. What is the effect for you as a reader of seeing similar characters and events repeated over the course of the book? Can you think of any other examples of doubling in literature?
6. Why is Kenya the one subject that Sullivan and his father can agree on? How does her adoption into the family help Teddy and Tip understand Sullivan and what he went through growing up?
7. Towards the end of the story we see images of four mothers (including the Virgin Mary) on Kenya's dresser. What is the author saying about women and mothers to have them all there together?
8. Why does Kenya's mother conceal her true identity from her daughter? Do you think that she imagines the conversation in the hospital with Tennessee Alice Moser after surgery or do you think it really happened?
9. What does Father Sullivan's encounter with Tennessee in the hospital suggest about his ability to heal?
10. Doyle is very invested in politics on both local and national levels, but he falters at the idea of taking home a stray child. What does this book say to you about social responsibility?
11. Of the many characters in *Run*, which did you feel most connected to on an emotional level? How do you explain that connection?
12. How did you react to Bernard Doyle's decision to bestow the heirloom statue on Kenya, a daughter who has literally shared nothing with his former wife, Bernadette? Do you think he made the same decision his wife would have made?

THE SAFETY OF SECRETS

AUTHOR: *DeLauné Michel*

PUBLISHER: Avon A, May 2008

WEBSITE: www.avonbooks.com
www.delaunemichel.com

AVAILABLE IN:
Trade Paperback, 320 pages, $13.95
ISBN: 978-0-060-81736-7

SUBJECT: Family/Relationships/
Coming of Age (Fiction)

"DeLauné Michel has written a terrifically funny book with a very tender heart. It manages to be wonderfully confessional and psychologically mysterious. The Safety of Secrets is the perfect curl-up-on-the-couch-and-read-all-day-long kind of book. It stays with you." —**Jill A. Davis, author of *Ask Again Later* and *Girls' Poker Night***

"Funny and touching, this is a tale of childhood—and how it never ends." —**Cathleen Schine, *New York Times* bestselling author of *The New Yorkers***

SUMMARY: "Now we're just alike." So begins Fiona and Patricia's friendship that warm autumn morning in first grade in Lake Charles, Louisiana, their bond forged ever closer by Fiona's abusive mother and Patricia's neglectful one. Their relationship is a source of continuity and strength through their move to L.A. to become actresses; through Fiona's marriage and Patricia's sudden fame. When husband and career pressures exact a toll, the women wonder if their friendship can survive. Then a dark secret from their past emerges, threatening to destroy not only their bond, but all they've worked for as well.

ABOUT THE AUTHOR: **DeLauné Michel** was raised in South Louisiana in a literary family. She has worked as an actor in theater, television, and film. She is the founding producer of Spoken Interludes, a salon-style reading series where award-winning, bestselling, and up-and-coming writers read their own work. Through Spoken Interludes, she has developed, has taught in, and continues to run outreach writing programs for at-risk teenagers.

1. Lifelong friendships are treasured for the great joy that they bring. But they also bring great pain. Do you find yourself choosing sides with either Fiona or Patricia?

2. Why do you think Patricia is drawn to Fiona? And why does Patricia remain friends with Fiona?

3. When Fiona finds out that she is pregnant, she goes to Patricia's home to tell her. She then lies to Neil that she didn't tell Patricia the news. Is Fiona's loyalty with Patricia appropriate? Does this loyalty justify Fiona's lying?

4. Why does Fiona cut her hair? To defy her mother or something else?

5. Before Fiona cut her hair, kids at school were already teasing her about her red hair. After she cuts it, she is even more afraid of what they will say. Should Patricia have tried to stop Fiona from getting it cut?

6. Why does Fiona's mother become so enraged when she gets her haircut? Is it only because Fiona broke her rule or is it something else?

7. How does the punishment that Fiona's mother comes up with set Fiona up for what happens to her at the end of the summer? Or does it?

8. Once Fiona is visibly pregnant, the way she is perceived in the world changes. How much of that is a reality and how much is her own thinking? Did her experience after the haircut make her more sensitive to this?

9. Fiona struggles with how she sees herself once she is pregnant and motherhood is looming. How does her relationship with her mother play into that?

10. Did Fiona learn to keep secrets as a way to get through life from her mother or did she learn it as a defense from her mother?

11. Why doesn't Fiona's father ever intervene?

12. Patricia defends telling their secret by telling Fiona that "It came out. I didn't plan for it to, it just did. But it's not like anyone knew it was you." How much ownership did Patricia have of that secret? Was it her right to tell it when she wanted to?

13. Patricia asks Fiona the one question that Fiona has never wanted to face since that eventful summer. "Why didn't you?" Was that the best thing for Fiona to hear or the worst?

14. Fiona and Patricia both came from abusive homes: Fiona emotionally and Patricia physically. How did each of their personalities develop in relation to those environments? And how did their careers and lives in Hollywood change who they are?

15. What does *The Safety of Secrets* reveal about the strength and fragility of human relationships?

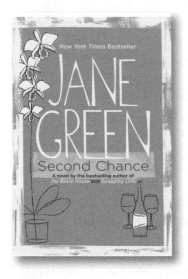

SECOND CHANCE

AUTHOR: *Jane Green*

PUBLISHER: Plume Books, May 2008

WEBSITE: www.plumebooks.com
www.janegreen.com

AVAILABLE IN:
Trade Paperback, 400 pages, $15.00
ISBN: 978-0-452-28944-4

SUBJECT: Relationships/Identity/
Personal Discovery (Fiction)

"Inspiring." —People magazine

"Green's many fans will revel in her interwoven plots."
—Entertainment Weekly

"Peopled with her trademark likable, sympathetic characters, Green's latest is sure to have wide appeal." —Booklist

SUMMARY: Apart for twenty years, school friends Paul, Saffron, Olivia, and Holly are in very different places in their lives when they get together in London after the death of a close friend, but through their rediscovered friendship they find new paths to follow and—despite some missteps along the way—begin to understand what it means to get a second chance.

In *Second Chance*, Jane Green follows the lives of these four as they help one another along, providing a lighthearted, warm, and witty look at contemporary middle age. By turns hilarious and moving, Green's new novel is an addictive read for women of any age and an insightful exploration of the possibilities that life holds for all of us.

ABOUT THE AUTHOR: **Jane Green** was a disaster at university, discovered writing soon afterward, and went on throughout her twenties to work as a journalist for various national newspapers and magazines in her hometown of London. *Straight Talking*, her (allegedly) largely autobiographical first novel, became a huge bestseller. Jane is currently at work on her tenth novel. She lives with her four children in Connecticut.

1. How does the title, *Second Chance*, relate to each of the main characters? How has their renewed friendship influenced each of their lives?

2. Although it was under tragic circumstances, Tom's death brought a lot of people together—not only the old friends from school but also Will, Tom's parents, Sarah, and others. Can you think of a similar instance in your own life when an unfortunate or terrible event led to a positive outcome? What were some of these positive outcomes?

3. In *Second Chance*, each character has a different understanding of what marriage means and how it works (or doesn't work) in their life. Which characters' marriages reflect aspects of your own relationships, past or current, and how?

4. Holly gets caught up in a tentative relationship with Will, despite her marriage to Marco. What is it about Will's and Holly's personalities that would draw them together? What do you think about the way things end up between them?

5. Green writes, "The problem with grief is that it doesn't go away. As time ticks on, the rawness dissipates somewhat, and you find yourself settling in to the pain, becoming accustomed to it, wearing it around your shoulders like an old, heavy scarf." What are your thoughts on this sentiment? How does this description of grief relate to your own experiences of loss and sadness?

6. The rediscovered friendship between these four characters gives each of them the chance to reflect on their lives over the past twenty years: the choices they've made, the regrets they have, the things they might have done differently. Think about your own life and things in your past that you wish you could change. How difficult do you think it is to make a significant change in your own life, or in the lives of your friends, for the future?

7. Saffron and Paul have both chosen lives that, to different extents, put them in the spotlight. How does the public's opinion affect each of them? Are there any decisions either of them makes that you would have dealt with differently?

8. What do you think of Olivia's trepidation before her blind date with Fred? What reasons did she have for being so nervous?

9. Over the twenty years that the four main characters were apart, each of them stayed in touch with Tom but not with one another. However, his death affected them in a way that none of them had expected. What do you think each of the characters' lives will be like after the book ends? Will they all stay in touch? Discuss how you envision each of them five or ten years later.

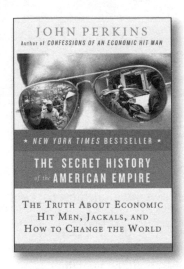

THE SECRET HISTORY OF THE AMERICAN EMPIRE

The Truth About Economic Hit Men, Jackals, and How to Change the World

AUTHOR: *John Perkins*

PUBLISHER: Plume Books, April 2008

WEBSITE: www.plumebooks.com
www.johnperkins.org

AVAILABLE IN:
Trade Paperback, 384 pages, $15.00
ISBN: 978-0-452-28957-4

SUBJECT: American History/Culture and World Issues/History (Nonfiction)

"A sweeping, bold assault on the tyranny of corporate globalization, full of drama and adventure, with devastating stories of greed run wild. But Perkins is undaunted, and offers imaginative ideas for a different world."
—**Howard Zinn, author of** A People's History of the United States

SUMMARY: The issues that John Perkins tackles in his new book, *The Secret History of the American Empire*, are both broader and more challenging than those described in his first bestseller, *Confessions of an Economic Hit Man*. Perkins makes an appeal for personal action by everyone who reads his book.

Despite the genuinely horrifying nature of many of the events Perkins describes, he remains optimistic about the possibility that conscientious individuals can help stop the corporatocracy's domination of other cultures and its disregard of the planet's environmental future. He explores how nongovernment organizations and nonprofit organizations worldwide are countering the actions of the corporatocracy, and provides a list of specific actions that individuals can take to thwart the corporatocracy and achieve a sustainable and peaceful world for all its citizens.

ABOUT THE AUTHOR: **John Perkins** is founder and president of the Dream Change Coalition, which works closely with Amazonian and other indigenous people to help preserve their environments and cultures. From 1971 to 1981 he worked for the international consulting firm of Chas. T. Main, where he became chief economist and director of economics and regional planning. Perkins has lectured and taught at universities and learning centers on four continents and is a regular lecturer for the Omega Center.

1. Do you agree with Perkins' statement that the corporatocracy is in fact an empire? If so, why? If not, why not?

2. Perkins' characterization of Hugo Chavez, president of Venezuela, is markedly different from the way he has been depicted in the mainstream media. How do you account for these differences? Which, if either, characterization do you find more plausible? Why?

3. The United States' war in Iraq is now in its fifth year. Perkins considers this war more dangerous to U.S. interests abroad than was the Vietnam war—he describes the Iraq war as a "clash of ideologies" rather than simply a regional conflict. What is your position on the Iraq war? Which, if any, of Perkins' opinions on the subject do you find valid? Why?

4. Perkins contends that the Central Intelligence Agency and the National Security Agency, which report to the executive branch of the United States government, authorized and in some cases carried out a number of assassinations of democratically elected leaders in Latin America and Africa who had refused to allow the corporatocracy to continue to do business as usual. Do you believe that any of these allegations are true? If so, why? If not, why not?

5. Do you believe that the resources of foreign countries should be fair game for acquisition by those with the most money and/or political clout?

6. Which of the incidents that Perkins describes in his book do you find the most disturbing? Why?

7. Several places in the book, Perkins states that male domination of the corporatocracy leads to its indiscriminate raping and pillaging of Third World cultures and the environment. He describes the attitudes of the Shuar people of the Amazon, who believe that men are responsible for hunting, gathering firewood, and protecting their people from threatening tribes, and women are responsible for raising children, growing crops, looking after the home, and telling the men when they need to stop what they are doing. Do you think that giving women more say in running corporations, governments, and the media would improve the quality of life for the planet's inhabitants? Why or why not?

8. Perkins ends his book with a list of actions individuals can take to thwart the corporatocracy and bring about a more just and peaceful world. Interestingly, most of the items on his list are also recommended by organizations that strive to protect the environment and produce sustainable energy and agricultural resources. Why do you suppose this is so? What, if any, of the actions Perkins lists are you prepared to undertake yourself? Why?

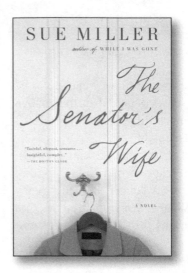

THE SENATOR'S WIFE

AUTHOR: *Sue Miller*

PUBLISHER: Vintage Books, January 2009

WEBSITE: www.ReadingGroupCenter.com

AVAILABLE IN:
Trade Paperback, 320 pages, $14.95
ISBN: 978-0-307-27669-8

SUBJECT: Family/Relationships/Women's Lives (Fiction)

"Pure Miller . . . tasteful, elegant, sensuous . . . insightful, complex . . . The Senator's Wife *is Miller's latest extended contemplation of marriage, and a master class in the refinement of craft."* —**The Boston Globe**

"Miller plays her hand in a masterly fashion." —**The New York Times Book Review**

SUMMARY: Meri is newly married, pregnant, and standing on the cusp of her life as a wife and mother, recognizing with some terror the gap between reality and expectation. Delia Naughton—wife of the two-term liberal senator Tom Naughton—is Meri's new neighbor in the adjacent New England town house. Delia's husband's chronic infidelity has been an open secret in Washington circles, but despite the complexity of their relationship, the bond between them remains strong. What keeps people together, even in the midst of profound betrayal? How can a journey imperiled by, and sometimes indistinguishable from, compromise and disappointment culminate in healing and grace? Delia and Meri find themselves leading strangely parallel lives, both reckoning with the contours and mysteries of marriage, one refined and abraded by years of complicated intimacy, the other barely begun.

ABOUT THE AUTHOR: **Sue Miller** is the best-selling author of the novels *Lost in the Forest, The World Below, While I Was Gone, The Distinguished Guest, For Love, Family Pictures*, and *The Good Mother*; the story collection *Inventing the Abbots*; and the memoir *The Story of My Father*. She lives in Boston, Massachussetts.

1. Have you read any of Sue Miller's other works? What shared themes, if any, do you see in her new novel?

2. Why do you think Miller called her novel *The Senator's Wife* when Meri's story gets equal time?

3. How does Meri's childhood, and specifically her relationship with her own mother, influence her relationship with Delia?

4. After Delia's first encounter with Nathan, what is her perception of him and his attitude towards Meri? Do you think she's right?

5. Meri seems to take great pleasure in keeping secrets. Why do you think that is? How does it help her, and how does it harm her? Ultimately, is it good for her marriage?

6. Meri tells Nathan about the effect Delia has on her. Discuss the idea of aperçus—why do you think Meri is so shaken by Delia's statements? Have you ever known someone who has a similar effect on you?

7. At times there are parallels between Meri and Tom, Delia and Nathan, and at other times the pairings are rearranged. Who do you think is most similar? Most unlike each other? Who would you most like to spend time with, if these were real people?

8. What purpose does the 50-page flashback serve? What do we learn about these characters that we might not know otherwise?

9. Meri has a difficult time accepting her pregnancy and motherhood. How do you think Miller feels about the character she created?

10. Delia's relationships with her grown children are quite varied. Why do you think she wound up with three such different results? What kind of mother was she?

11. Discuss Delia and Tom's relationship. Who has the most power, and how is it wielded? What would you have done in Delia's place at these key junctures: When she found out about Carolee; when Tom had his stroke; when she walked in on Tom and Meri?

For the complete Reading Group Guide, visit ReadingGroupCenter.com.

SLAVE
My True Story

AUTHOR: *Mende Nazer* and *Damien Lewis*

PUBLISHER: PublicAffairs, April 2005

WEBSITE: www.publicaffairsbooks.com

AVAILABLE IN:
Trade Paperback, 352 pages, $12.00
ISBN: 978-1-58648-318-0

SUBJECT: Culture & World Issues/
Inspiration/Women's Lives (Memoir)

"Harrowing." —People **Magazine**

"Beautiful and at times heart-wrenching." —The Washington Post

*"Slave constitutes an act of tremendous courage. A solitary and profoundly moving voice emerging from the most silenced of quarters." —***Monica Ali, author of** *Brick Lane*

SUMMARY: At age twelve, Mende Nazer lost her childhood. It began one horrific night in 1993, when Arab raiders swept through her Nuba village, setting fire to the village huts and murdering the adults. The raiders rounded up thirty-one young children, including Mende, who was eventually sold to a wealthy Arab family in Sudan's capital city, Khartoum. So began Mende's seven dark years of enslavement. Normally, Mende's story never would have come to light, but when she was sent to work for another master—a diplomat working in London—she made a dramatic break for freedom.

Published to critical acclaim for the honesty and clarity of its prose, *Slave* is a story almost beyond belief. It depicts the strength and dignity of the Nuba tribe. It recounts the savage cruelty of the secret, modern-day trade in slaves. Most of all, it is a remarkable testimony to one young woman's unbreakable spirit and tremendous courage.

ABOUT THE AUTHOR: **Mende Nazer** was granted political asylum by the British government in 2003. She currently lives in London. **Damien Lewis** is a British journalist who has reported widely from Sudan and helped Mende escape. He lives in Dublin, Ireland.

1. Were you aware that there is a modern day slave trade? Why do you think it gets so little attention? Is there something that can be done to increase awareness?

2. How does Mende's practice of Islam compare to your own prior knowledge or common stereotypes of the religion? How is her captors' faith different from Mende's?

3. What role do family and tradition play in Nuba identity? Do you think Mende had a happy childhood and, if so, how does it sustain and nurture her during her traumatic years as a slave?

4. Mende was circumcised when she was very young, which she describes as a traumatic and painful event. Is female circumcision, controversially termed female genital mutilation, a practice that requires outside intervention, or is it a custom that outsiders do not understand and should not interfere with?

5. How do Mende's experiences as a slave affect her self-worth? Why did Mende lie about her situation to those who might have helped her?

6. How is Mende seen as a commodity by Rahab's female friends and by her husband's male friends? Is their treatment of her different based on gender?

7. What shocked you most about Mende's experience as a slave? Were the physical or psychological abuses that Mende suffered more difficult for you to read?

8. Mende's account, while horrifying, does at times present a comical view of a tribal girl encountering the modern world for the first time. Did her reactions make you view your own culture and lifestyle differently?

9. Mende's choice to write this book created significant consequences for her, her friends and her family. Would you have made a similar sacrifice in order to give a voice to the slaves who remain in captivity?

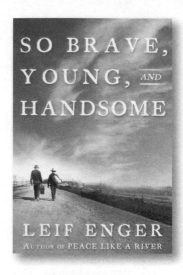

SO BRAVE, YOUNG, AND HANDSOME

AUTHOR: *Leif Enger*

PUBLISHER: Atlantic Monthly Press
April 2008

WEBSITE: www.leif-enger.com
www.groveatlantic.com

AVAILABLE IN:
Hardcover, 304 pages, $24.00
ISBN: 978-0-87113-985-6

SUBJECT: Adventure/American History/
Family (Fiction)

A Book Sense Pick

"An inviting voice guides readers through this expansive saga of redemption in the early twentieth century West and gives a teeming vitality to [the] period. . . . Peopled with sharply carved characters and splendid surprises. . . . An adventure story . . . so rich you can smell the spilled whiskey and feel the grit." —**Publisher's Weekly**

"[Leif Enger is] in fine storytelling form, as he spins a picaresque tale of redemption and renewal amid the fading glories of the Old West." —**Kirkus Reviews** (starred review)

SUMMARY: One of *Time* magazine's top-five novels of the year and a *New York Times* best seller, Leif Enger's first novel, *Peace Like a River*, captured readers' hearts around the nation. His new novel is a stunning successor—a touching, nimble, and rugged story of an aging train robber on a quest to reconcile the claims of love and judgment on his life, and the failed writer who goes with him. With its smooth mix of romanticism and gritty reality, *So Brave, Young, and Handsome* often recalls the Old West's greatest cowboy stories. But it is also about an ordinary man's determination as he risks everything in order to understand what it's all worth, and follows an unlikely dream in the hope it will lead him back home.

ABOUT THE AUTHOR: **Leif Enger** is the author of *Peace Like a River*. He was raised in Osakis, Minnesota, and worked as a reporter and producer for Minnesota Public Radio for nearly twenty years. Enger lives in Minnesota with his wife and two sons.

1. What elements of Enger's book play off the conventions of cowboy movies and cowboy novels?

2. How does Enger make these outsized characters convincing?

3. Talk about love in the book, relationships that occur or are recalled.

4. Describe Glendon as a phenomenon. What are traits you hold onto? Is it his melting disappearances? How are both Siringo and Glendon almost phoenixes, myths that resurface despite the odds?

5. In contrast to the romance of heroic exploits, what are some blasts of reality? What are other times Monte and his cohorts are battered by weather, hunger, or assailants? Is the life of the outlaw worthwhile?

6. If you were to cast this book as a movie, who would play the principal roles? What would be essential scenes? As a director, how would you handle the frame tale of Monte, Susannah, and Redstart

7. Is it justice that Glendon is seeking in the novel? For whom? Do you think it is achieved? Is forgiveness as important as justice in the book?

8. The novel's humor is sometimes ironic or deadpan, other times pure slapstick. What purpose does recurrent comedy serve in a story with such violence and loss?

9. What is the time of the novel? Enger gives us a date, but what are other clues? Driving with pride eighty miles in a day? Pancho Villa?

10. How do books pervade the novel?

11. "Most men are hero and devil," says Siringo. Does that statement hold true in the book? And in general?

12. How is Darlys the Sharpshooter a pivotal figure? Think about her deft explosion of the glass orb in Monte's hand as well as her well practiced aim later at Siringo who has cruelly spurned her.

13. "Say what you like about melodrama, it beats confusion." Is this how we feel after reading a page-turner? Enger's book has ambiguity to spare, but are you in doubt at the end about events or characters?

14. Where do our sympathies lie in *So Brave, Young, and Handsome*? Did you feel a loss as Hood sank deeper into runaway crime? Is everyone on the trail tainted except maybe Monte? Is he, as well?

15. Do you see an analogy with Don Quixote and Sancho Panza in the book? (There are even recurrent windmills!) Can you talk about the idea of the Quest? The idealism, as well as the consistent blanket of reality? Give examples?

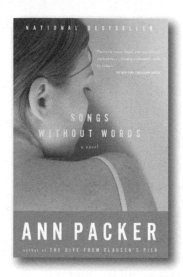

SONGS WITHOUT WORDS

AUTHOR: *Ann Packer*

PUBLISHER: Vintage Books, July 2008

WEBSITE: www.ReadingGroupCenter.com
www.annpacker.com

AVAILABLE IN:
Trade Paperback, 384 pages, $14.95
ISBN: 978-0-375-72717-7

SUBJECT: Relationships/Family/
Women's Lives (Fiction)

"Songs Without Words is an eloquent, on occasion harrowing account of friendship and its limits, the mind and its fatal fragilities, and the saving graces of human nature. Packer captures mental pathologies exceptionally well and writes beautifully about despair and love and how they travel together throughout a lifetime." —**Kay Redfield Jamison, author of** *An Unquiet Mind*

SUMMARY: Liz and Sarabeth were girlhood neighbors in the suburbs of Northern California, brought as close as sisters by the suicide of Sarabeth's mother. In the decades that followed, their relationship remained a source of continuity and strength. But when Liz's adolescent daughter enters dangerous waters, the women's friendship takes a devastating turn, forcing Liz and Sarabeth to question their most deeply held beliefs about their connection. From the bestselling author of *The Dive from Clausen's Pier*, *Songs Without Words* is the gripping story of a lifelong friendship pushed to the breaking point.

ABOUT THE AUTHOR: **Ann Packer** received the Great Lakes Book Award for *The Dive from Clausen's Pier*, which was a national bestseller. She is also the author of *Mendocino and Other Stories*. She is a past recipient of a James Michener award and a National Endowment for the Arts fellowship. Her fiction has appeared in *The New Yorker, Ploughshares*, and other magazines, as well as in *Prize Stories 1992: The O. Henry Awards*. She lives in northern California with her family.

1. Ann Packer has been praised for the lifelike quality of her fiction. Do you feel that the friendship depicted here seems especially true to life? Do you find yourself choosing sides with either Liz or Sarabeth?

2. Why does Lauren attempt to kill herself? What are the immediate and the more suppressed causes? How does Lauren herself explain it?

3. Liz tells Brody that she feels completely guilty for Lauren's suicide attempt. "I know, it sounds crazy," she says, "but the point is: if it was your fault, then you weren't powerless—you weren't at the mercy of stuff just happening." To which Brody replies: "You're always going to be at the mercy of stuff just happening, no matter what." What different ways of looking at life do these two positions represent? To what extent are they "at the mercy of stuff just happening"?

4. Thinking back over her relationship with her daughter, Liz imagines herself "bowing to Lauren, acknowledging Lauren." Had she somehow failed to do that? She couldn't think of anything more important for a mother to do." Why would nothing be more important than this kind of acknowledgment of one's child? Why does Liz choose the word "bowing"?

5. After Lauren has returned from the hospital, Liz admits to Lauren that she and Sarabeth are "having some problems." After that, Lauren occasionally asks her mother about her relationship with Sarabeth. Do you think Lauren is intentionally pressuring Liz to talk to her? Do you think it's Lauren's place to pressure her mother about Sarabeth?

6. Liz and Sarabeth have a long history together. Do you think that, without Lauren's attempted suicide, Liz and Sarabeth would have ended up in the same place anyway?

7. Why do you think Lauren is drawn to Sarabeth? Do you think it has more to do with Sarabeth's experience with depression and suicide, or with Sarabeth's knowledge of art and her less-conventional life? Or something else entirely?

For the complete Reading Group Guide, visit ReadingGroupCenter.com.

SOUL

AUTHOR: *Tobsha Lerner*

PUBLISHER: Forge, May 2008

WEBSITE: www.tor-forge.com

AVAILABLE IN:
Trade Paperback, 432 pages, $14.95
ISBN: 978-0-7653-2010-0

SUBJECT: Intrigue/Fantasy/Romance
(Fiction)

"A riveting page-turner." —***Publishers Weekly*** **on** ***The Witch of Cologne***

"The kind of all-consuming novel that readers hate to see end." —***Booklist*** **on** ***The Witch of Cologne***

"Deep and moving." —***Romantic Times BOOKreviews*** **on** ***The Witch of Cologne***

SUMMARY: In 19th century Britain, Lavinia is married to an older man who seems to appreciate her lively curiosity. Lavinia proves to be an apt pupil in both the study and the bedroom, glorying in the pleasures of the physical. In 21st-century Los Angeles, geneticist Julia is trying to identify people who can kill without remorse. Stunned to discover that she seems to possess the trait she is looking for, Julia is reassured of her emotions by her intense passion for her husband and her delight in her pregnancy. In the past, Lavinia's desire for her husband grows, but his cools as he becomes fascinated with another. In the present, Julia's love overwhelms her husband, who leaves her. Lavinia and Julia feel the tortures of passion unspent. Cold logic tells them that the deaths of their tormentors will bring them peace. Separated by a hundred years, two Huntington women face the same decision. Their choices will echo far into the future.

ABOUT THE AUTHOR: **Tobsha Learner** is a renowned playwright and short story writer whose works have been performed and published throughout the world. She was born and raised in London, England, where she trained to be a sculptor.

1. Learner draws an historical comparison between phrenology and genetics, Darwin and creationism, the onset of the American Civil War and the fall-out of contemporary American Foreign policy—do you think by raising such comparisons she is commenting on the nature of progress or suggesting history in some ways merely repeats itself?

2. *Soul* is very much a story about power. What are the greatest differences between Julia and Lavinia in terms of the types of power that they have, or lack, in the world—intellectual, familial, social, economic, professional, and maternal?

3. Learner's characters talk frequently about nature vs. nurture, about genetic imperatives vs. free will and moral responsibility. Is Lavinia a moral person?

4. Why do you think that Julia is able to avoid killing Klaus—and therefore avoid either going to jail or losing her own life—while Lavinia is compelled to kill James? Do you think that Lavinia's decision was the right one, either morally or in terms of her struggle for survival? Does Julia represent a more evolved version of her great-grandmother, or does she simply have more choices?

5. Post-traumatic Stress Disorder has a huge impact not only on combat soldiers but also their families and friends. The notion of genetically profiling men who would not suffer from it is morally complex—how does Learner address this issue?

6. Learner portrays Klaus as someone who has frequently failed to stand up for himself, yet when he leaves Julia, he does so in an aggressive and self-centered way. Is he actually a narcissist, or simply someone who took years to learn how to prioritize his own needs? Is he a modern-day cad? How does he compare with James, his parallel in Lavinia's story?

7. What do you think of Julia's decision, early on in the book, to accept the Defense Department contract? Is she ethical in her thinking about her work? Can you envision situations in which her super-soldiers could be essential to public safety or national security? How do you feel about her decisions at the book's end?

8. Gabriel is an enigmatic character. Do you think that he loves Julia, or does he seduce her for professional gain? Given their age difference, what do you make of the fact that he genuinely seems to care about her well-being? How does this relate to his own up-bringing?

9. The Irish Famine was one of the great crimes perpetuated by an indifferent England—in what way were the English aristocracy implicated?

Photo: © Elena Seibert

SOUVENIR

AUTHOR: *Therese Fowler*

PUBLISHER: Ballantine Books, February 2009

WEBSITE: www.thereaderscircle.com

AVAILABLE IN:
Trade Paperback, 400 pages, $14.00
ISBN: 978-0-345-49969-1

SUBJECT: Family/Relationships/
Women's Lives (Fiction)

"Fowler's debut is the heartbreaking story of a woman who made what she thought was a responsible decision, only to have to live with the consequences. . . . When Meg discovers she has amyotrophic lateral sclerosis (ALS), she knows she has only one chance to make peace with the past and give her daughter hope for the future. The choices made by Meg and Savannah may be controversial with some readers, but, nevertheless, this outstanding debut is recommended." —**Library Journal** (**starred review**)

SUMMARY: Meg Powell and Carson McKay were raised side by side on their families' farms, bonded by a love that only deepened. Everyone in their small rural community in northern Florida thought that Meg and Carson would always be together. But at twenty-one, Meg was presented with a marriage proposal she could not refuse, forever changing the course of her life. Seventeen years later, Meg's marriage has become routine, and she spends her time juggling the demands of her medical practice, the needs of her widowed father, and the whims of her rebellious teenage daughter, Savannah, who is confronting her burgeoning sexuality in a dangerous manner, and pushing her mother away just when she needs her most. Then, after a long absence, Carson returns home to prepare for his wedding to a younger woman. As Carson struggles to determine where his heart and future lie, Meg makes a shocking discovery that will upset the balance of everyone around her.

ABOUT THE AUTHOR: **Therese Fowler** holds an MFA in creative writing. She grew up in Illinois, and now lives in Raleigh, North Carolina, with her husband and two sons. This is her first novel.

1. Did Meg realistically have a choice about whether or not to marry Brian? Even if her parents pressured her into it for reasons of their own, was anything stopping her from refusing?

2. Meg sacrifices her happiness for the sake of her parents . . . But do you think she embraces the role of martyr a little too zealously? And do you think the prospect of attending med school and becoming a doctor entered into her decision at all?

3. Does Meg ever come to grips with the fact that her parents have betrayed her by pressuring her into a loveless marriage solely for financial gain? How does this affect the kind of woman she becomes, as wife and mother?

4. Is there a chance that Meg's decision to marry Brian had something to do with her feelings for Carson? Is there evidence in the novel that she was afraid of the intensity of those feelings and was looking for a way out? What other reasons, besides what Meg consciously believes, could have influenced her decision?

5. William Faulkner once wrote, "The past isn't dead. It isn't even past." How do those lines pertain to *Souvenir*?

6. Did Carson give up on Meg too easily back in 1989? What more could he have done to win her back?

7. Are Meg and Carson trapped by the past? Are their memories and regrets preventing them from moving forward?

8. Do you think Carson and Meg find some peace and happiness by the novel's end? What has the price of that been for them and for those close to them? Was it worth it?

9. Did you find Meg to be a likable character? Why or why not?

10. How would you face a diagnosis of ALS, or Lou Gehrig's Disease? Do you think Meg makes the right choice, or is her decision to take her own life a selfish one?

11. Does Carson do the right thing by breaking off his engagement with Val? Isn't he treating her the same way that Meg treated him years earlier?

12. What do you think made Savannah so vulnerable to Kyle's advances and to his introduction of drugs and sex into their relationship?

13. Does *Souvenir* accurately portray the dangers of the Internet, or does it exaggerate the threats?

14. Is Meg a good mother? How does her relationship to her own mother color her relationship with Savannah?

THE SPACE BETWEEN BEFORE AND AFTER

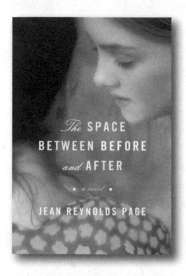

AUTHOR: *Jean Reynolds Page*

PUBLISHER: Avon A, May 2008

WEBSITE: www.avonbooks.com
www.jeanreynoldspage.com

AVAILABLE IN:
Trade Paperback, 416 pages, $13.95
ISBN: 978-0-061-45218-5

SUBJECT: Family/Personal Challenges/
Relationships (Fiction)

"[A] complex, multi-layered book. [Page] seamlessly navigates the book's intertwining narratives and presents believable characters, at once imperfect and utterly sympathetic. Both the story's emotional pull and intricate plot twists are sure to seduce new readers." —Publishers Weekly

"Page portrays these past and present emotional quagmires with an acutely intuitive eye, drawing the reader into the complicated lives of her sympathetic characters." —Booklist

SUMMARY: Forty-two and divorced, Holli Templeton has begun to realize the pleasures of owning her life for the first time. But when she learns that her son Conner has unexpectedly fled college and moved to Texas with his troubled girlfriend Kilian and she begins to note signs of decline in her beloved grandmother, Holli realizes she must once again put her family's needs before her own.

In the tight space between these two generations, Holli's journey back to Texas stirs unresolved hurts from her childhood. But something else happens in this uneasy homecoming. Comfort arrives in the ethereal presence of the mother long lost to her. The space between before and after—easily the most challenging place she has ever known—begins to reveal an unanticipated hope for what the future might hold.

ABOUT THE AUTHOR: **Jane Reynolds Page** is also the author of *A Blessed Event* and *Accidental Happiness*. She grew up in North Carolina and graduated with a degree in journalism from The University of North Carolina at Chapel Hill. She lives with her husband and children in the Seattle area.

1. Kilian, a young woman living with cystic fibrosis, is a central character in the novel. In what ways does learning of this condition alter Holli's response to her son's relationship with Kilian? How would you react if your child became involved with someone living with a serious medical condition?

2. When she marries Harrison, Hollyanne changes her name to Holli. Why did she make this decision and what is she trying to accomplish? Do you think she succeeds?

3. What individual motivations draw Raine and Georgia together in friendship? How does the relationship evolve with time? Is Holli right to resent Raine's attachment to Georgia?

4. When the facts of Celia's death are revealed to Holli by Grandma Raine, they absolve Georgia, and to a certain extent Ray, of responsibility for the loss of Celia and the baby. Even in light of this, Holli cannot let go of her anger toward Georgia. What other factors play into Holli's feelings about her stepmother? Are they valid?

5. Holli is terribly upset when she learns of Kilian's pregnancy. She has great concern over the impact a baby would have on Conner's life, and she admits to herself that she wants there to be some "medical, if not moral" reason for the pregnancy to be terminated. Given this, why is she devastated by the news that Kilian has ended the pregnancy?

6. Why did Kilian lie about having the abortion? Do you think she did this to protect Conner, or were her reasons self-serving?

7. How do you feel about Grandma Raine's "visitations" with her lost daughter and, likewise, Holli's occasional, strong sense of her mother's presence? Do you believe that spiritual elements of those we love remain among us?

8. How responsible is Harrision for the break-up of his marriage to Holli? Did Holli's childhood baggage drive the demise of their relationship, or were her reactions to Harrison's behavior in the marriage appropriate?

9. In spite of the fact that Tina was the result of Ray's infidelity with Georgia, Holli adores her stepsister and develops a life-long bond with the younger woman. What accounts for Holli's lack of resentment—and in fact her abiding devotion—towards a sibling who was the product of such painful circumstances?

10. Significant events in Holli's family run parallel with flashpoints involving human exploration in space. How do you think the triumphs and tragedies of NASA affect us as a nation? What do they represent in our cultural identity?

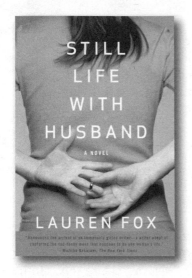

STILL LIFE WITH HUSBAND

AUTHOR: *Lauren Fox*

PUBLISHER: Vintage Books, April 2008

WEBSITE: www.ReadingGroupCenter.com

AVAILABLE IN:
Trade Paperback, 320 pages, $13.95
ISBN: 978-0-307-27737-4

SUBJECT: Women's Lives/Family/
Relationships (Fiction)

"A delightful new voice in American fiction, a voice that instantly recalls the wry, knowing prose of Lorrie Moore crossed with the screwball talents of the cartoonist Roz Chast." —**Michiko Kakutani, *The New York Times***

"Any woman who's ever found herself looking at her life and wondering how on earth she wound up there will relate to the characters in this funny, honest novel." —**Jodi Picoult, author of *Nineteen Minutes***

"Read Still Life with Husband *for its funny, winning voice and an ending that could be debated by book clubs for months to come."* —**Ann Oldenburg, *USA Today***

SUMMARY: Meet Emily Ross, thirty years old, married to her college sweetheart, and personal advocate for cake at breakfast time.

Meet Emily's husband, Kevin, a sweet technical writer with a passion for small appliances and a teary weakness for *Little Women*.

Enter David, a sexy young reporter with longish floppy hair and the kind of face Emily feels the weird impulse to lick.

In this captivating novel of marriage and friendship, Lauren Fox explores the baffling human heart and the dangers of getting what you wish for.

ABOUT THE AUTHOR: **Lauren Fox** earned her MFA from the University of Minnesota in 1998. Her work has appeared in *The New York Times, Utne, Seventeen, Glamour*, and *Salon*. She lives in Milwaukee with her husband and daughter. *Still Life with Husband* is her first novel.

1. What does Emily's dream in the opening scene say about Emily's state of mind, and her marriage? How effective is it as a prelude to the story that follows?

2. Emily and Meg joke that they want to start a girl group called 'N Secure. Emily suggests, "I'll be the drummer . . . but I'll just drum really quietly. And after every song we can kind of sidle up to the microphone and say, 'Was that okay?'." How would you characterize Emily's sense of humor? What scenes or passages do you find most funny in the novel?

3. In her conversation with Meg about Meg's pregnancy, Emily is ashamed to admit that she is unsure she'll ever be ready to have a baby. Why is this something Emily feels guilty about?

4. Discuss the scene in the café when Emily meets David. Is agreeing to meet him for coffee okay, or not okay? Is Meg right in saying "There's a line, you know, and it seemed like you crossed it"? What does Meg mean by "a line," and do you agree that Emily crossed it? How much freedom can, or should, married women have in this kind of situation?

5. How sympathetic a character is Kevin? Does he come across as a solid, dependable man who loves his wife? Or as a conventional, controlling person who wants to push Emily into a life she doesn't want? Noticing his reading material, *Sound Investments for the Careful Planner*, Emily feels "a familiar pang of love for my steady, staid husband. He's like a brick wall you can lean against when you're tired—immobile, rutted with predictable grooves, always there." What does this thought indicate about Emily's feelings toward Kevin?

6. Is Emily's friendship with Meg more important to her, in a sense, than her marriage to Kevin? What does the friendship suggest about women's bonds with each other as opposed to their bonds with their spouses?

7. Emily wonders whether her restlessness is caused by marriage itself: "Being married is like reading the same novel over and over again. You might discover new subtleties of language on the twenty-millionth read-through, a metaphor or two you'd missed before, but the plot is always the same. Kevin is in a bad mood, and there's nothing I can do about it: chapter six." Is Emily right about the inherent problems in marriage? If so, should she allow herself, at least briefly, the excitement of getting to know David?

For the complete Reading Group Guide, visit ReadingGroupCenter.com.

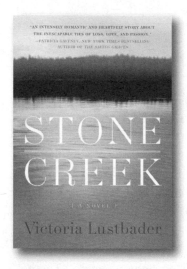

STONE CREEK

AUTHOR: *Victoria Lustbader*

PUBLISHER: Harper Paperbacks, May 2008

WEBSITE: www.harpercollins.com
www.victorialustbader.com

AVAILABLE IN:
Trade Paperback, 400 pages, $13.95
ISBN: 978-0-061-36921-6

SUBJECT: Relationships/Family/
Personal Discovery (Fiction)

"What You'll Love: The author's affection for her emotionally wounded characters is palpable and infectious, making it nearly impossible not to get invested in the plot." —Washington Post

"My heart truly ached for the protagonists in this poignant, affecting story about love, loss, being lost and finding your way." — **Elizabeth Noble, author of** *The Reading Group* **and** *Things I Want My Daughter to Know*

"An intensely romantic and heartfelt story of three fascinating people bound together by the inescapable ties of loss, love, and passion." —**Patricia Gaffney, author of** *The Saving Graces*

SUMMARY: Danny, a young widower, still grieves for his late wife, but for the sake of his five-year-old son, Caleb, he knows he must move on. Alone in her summer house, Lily has left her workaholic husband, Paul, to his long hours and late nights back in the city.

What occurs when Lily and Danny meet is immediate and undeniable. But ultimately it is little Caleb's sadness and need that will tip the scales, upsetting a precarious balance between joy and despair, between what cannot happen . . . and what must.

An unforgettable novel of tremendous emotional heft, *Stone Creek* brilliantly illuminates how the powers of love and loss transform the human heart.

ABOUT THE AUTHOR: **Victoria Lustbader**, a former book editor, became an author herself with her first novel, *Hidden*. She divides her time between Southampton, New York, and New York City.

1. Do you believe there can only be one true love? Or is it possible to love again with the same kind of depth and fulfillment?

2. Do you think infidelity is ever justified? Do you think its ever justified to act in opposition to your own sense of what's morally right?

3. Danny's loss is the most obvious; what loss do you think each of the other characters—Lily, Paul, Eve—suffer from? Do you think they all succeed in forgiving?

4. In reading about the beginning of their marriage, Lily's and Paul's relationship seems to be in perfect balance. How do you think this changes and what does Danny offer that Lily hasn't gotten in her relationship with Paul?

5. Danny believes that he and Tara would never have had the problems that Lily and Paul have. Do you agree? Why? What are the differences in the two relationships?

6. How do you grieve differently for a private loss rather than a public one? Do you think one process is easier than the other?

7. Lily's love for Danny is inextricably bound to her love and need for Caleb. Would she have fallen in love with Danny if he didn't have a son, or if she didn't yearn for a child?

8. Do you think that Danny was right to give Eve Tara's journal? What does his act say about his feelings toward Eve and about his grieving over Tara? What do you think Eve's reaction to what she reads would be?

9. Did Lily make the right decision in staying with Paul? What do you think would have happened if she had chosen Danny?

10. Lily and Danny will see one another again—they are determined not to lose their friendship, and Caleb's happiness. What do you think will happen when they do? Do you think it's possible for two people, who feel the way they do about each other, to remain just friends?

11. Is this a happy ending?

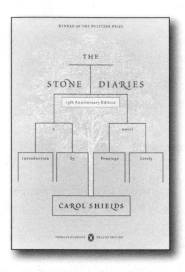

THE STONE DIARIES
15th Anniversary Edition

AUTHOR: *Carol Shields*

PUBLISHER: Penguin Classic
September 2008

WEBSITE: www.penguin.com

AVAILABLE IN:
Trade Paperback, 304 pages, $16.00
ISBN: 978-0-143-10550-3

SUBJECT: Women's Lives/Identity/Personal Discovery (Fiction)

"A kind of family album made into a work of art." —New York Newsday

SUMMARY: From her calamitous birth in Manitoba in 1905 to her journey with her father to Indiana, throughout her years as a wife, mother, and widow, Daisy Stone Goodwill struggled to understand her place in her own life. Now, in old age, Daisy attempts to tell her life story through a novel. How do small lives, the kind most women were once assumed to lead, assume significance and coherence? This is the problem that Carol Shields addresses in *The Stone Diaries*. How closely do our versions of those lives correspond to objective facts? Can facts be said to exist at all in the context of something as changeable and arbitrary as a life? To what extent do "our" stories really belong to us, considering the tendency that other people—parents, spouses, children—have to intrude in them, interpret them, claim them?

The Stone Diaries approaches these problems with seductive prose, a serene wit and an artfulness that is all the more dazzling given the novel's apparent insistence on the ordinary.

ABOUT THE AUTHOR: Before her death in 2003, **Carol Shields** was the author of several novels and short-story collections, including *The Orange Fish, Swann, Various Miracles, Happenstance*, and *The Republic of Love*. *The Stone Diaries* was nominated for the National Book Critics Circle Award and the 1993 Booker Prize, and won Canada's Governor General Award. It was also named one of the best books of the year by *Publishers Weekly* and a Notable Book by *The New York Times Book Review*.

1. The first chapter of this novel is the only one that is narrated entirely in the first person. Why might the author have chosen to shift narrative voices? At what points in the book does the narrative "I" return? Who do you think is telling Daisy's story?

2. What irony is implicit in the fact that Mercy Goodwill is unaware of her own pregnancy? Compare this near-virgin birth to Daisy's own catastrophically chaste honeymoon. How do this novel's female characters experience sex, pregnancy, and childbirth?

3. Although Daisy describes her mother as "extraordinarily obese" and taller than her husband, a photo reveals that Mercy Goodwill is actually shorter than Cuyler and no more than ordinarily husky. Is Daisy lying? Or does she merely have "a little trouble with getting things straight?" Where else are there discrepancies between Daisy's version of her life and the book's "documentation?"

4. Does *The Stone Diaries* subvert traditional sex roles? Where do Daisy and the novel's other female characters derive their greatest pleasure and fulfillment? How badly do Shields's women need men?

5. When Cuyler Goodwill loses his wife, he builds her a tower. When his daughter loses her first husband, she never tells the story to another soul. What might account for her reticence? How deeply does Daisy seem to love either of her husbands? On the other hand, how trustworthy are these characters' public displays of emotion?

6. What role does Daisy—or Carol Shields—assign "witnesses" like the Jewish peddler Abram Gozhd' Skutari, the bicyclist who kills Clarentine Flett, or Cuyler Goodwill's housekeeper? Why might these characters reappear in the narrative years after their initial entrances? How trustworthy are their interpretations of Daisy's life and character?

7. What role does memory play in *The Stone Diaries*? How much of Daisy's diary is remembered and how much is imagined?

8. In the chapter entitled "Sorrow," a number of characters offer explanations for Daisy's depression. How accurate are any of these? Are we given any reason to trust one interpretation over others? How well do any of Daisy's intimates really know her? How well does the reader know her by the book's close?

9. How does Daisy influence her children or determine the choices they make in their own lives? Is Daisy Flett a "good" mother, a "good" wife or daughter? Does *The Stone Diaries* allow us to make such easy judgments about its protagonist?

Photo: © Christina Pabst

THE STORY
OF FORGETTING

AUTHOR: *Stefan Merrill Block*

PUBLISHER: Random House Trade Paperbacks
April 2009

WEBSITE: www.thereaderscircle.com

AVAILABLE IN:
Trade Paperback, 320 pages, $14.00
ISBN: 978-0-8129-7982-4

SUBJECT: Personal Challenges/Family/
Social Issues (Fiction)

"A deeply felt novel . . . The Story of Forgetting *offers us both solace and illumination. Stefan Merrill Block possesses a singular mix of imagination, compassion, and scientific understanding; he is equally gifted at spinning fantastic tales as he is at bringing genetic histories to vivid life."*
——**Sarah Shun-lien Bynum, author of** *Madeleine Is Sleeping*

SUMMARY: Abel Haggard is an elderly hunchback who haunts the remnants of his family's farm in the encroaching shadow of the Dallas suburbs, adrift in recollections of those he loved and lost long ago. As a young man, he believed himself to be "the one person too many;" now he is all that remains. Hundreds of miles to the south, in Austin, Seth Waller is a teenage "Master of Nothingness"—a prime specimen of that gangly, pimple-rashed, too-smart breed of adolescent that vanishes in a puff of sarcasm at the slightest threat of human contact. When his mother is diagnosed with a rare form of early-onset Alzheimer's, Seth sets out on a quest to find her lost relatives and to conduct an "empirical investigation" that will uncover the truth of her genetic history. Though neither knows of the other's existence, Abel and Seth are linked by a dual legacy: the disease that destroys the memories of those they love and the story of Isidora—an edenic fantasy world free from the sorrows of remembrance, a land without memory where nothing is ever possessed, so nothing can be lost.

ABOUT THE AUTHOR: **Stefan Merrill Block** was born in 1982 and grew up in Plano, Texas. He graduated from Washington University in St. Louis in 2004. *The Story of Forgetting* is his first novel. He lives in Brooklyn.

1. The last words of the book are ". . . whatever she needed she had only to imagine." How is imagination a central and absolute necessity for the members of the Haggard family?

2. What is the relationship between the fables of Isidora and the rest of the book? How are situations, characters, and feelings from the lives of the Haggard family transformed in these fables? Why do you think that the Haggards maintain this storytelling tradition despite everything that they lose, forget, and abandon? What traditions do you keep that help maintain your own family's identity? How do your traditions relate to your family's history?

3. Comparing the Haggard family's two legacies–the EOA-23 gene and the stories of Isidora–the author writes: "Two ideas, spontaneously improvised, altering in slight ways with each passage, yet remaining, fundamentally, themselves." In what other ways are these two inheritances similar? What is the relationship between them? In what ways are they different?

4. When Jamie leaves home, she leaves a letter for Abel that claims, "life here is no longer possible." Do you think that if Abel hadn't told her the truth she would have been able to stay? Do you think that he was right to tell her?

5. Despite the horrors of Alzheimer's disease, are there ways in which its most well-known symptom, memory loss, is liberating for some of the characters in this book? What do you think of the possibility of there being something positive, even blissful, in the oblivion of Alzheimer's disease? In certain instances, might it be better to forget?

6. By the end of *The Story of Forgetting*, Jamie appears desperate to return to her childhood home. Do you think she would have still felt this need if she hadn't developed Alzheimer's disease? Was it only after she had forgotten the reasons she had left, and her guilt over abandoning Abel, that she could return? Do you think that eventually she would have returned anyway, even if her memory had not failed?

7. Why do you think that Paul, when he begins to develop Alzheimer's disease, so quickly forgets who Abel is, replacing him with the memory of Jamie Whitman? Do you think there is a way that Paul's love for his brother remains intact, even after he has forgotten who Abel is?

8. How is love stronger than memory loss in this book? How is it not? Do you think one's love is made more or less valid if one forgets and confuses its conditions?

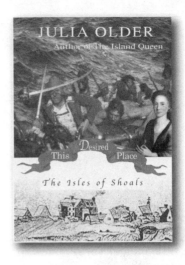

THIS DESIRED PLACE
The Isles of Shoals

AUTHOR: *Julia Older*

PUBLISHER: Appledore Books, January 2007

WEBSITE: www.AppledoreBooks.com

AVAILABLE IN:
Hardcover, 456 pages, $26.00
ISBN: 978-0-9741488-2-3

SUBJECT: Love & Loss /Personal Challenges/ Family (Historical Fiction)

"A rollicking adventure from cover to cover. Also highly recommended is the previous Shoals novel, The Island Queen.*" —Midwest Book Review*

"History comes to life on New England's storied Isles of Shoals—*an exciting blend of fact and fiction." —***David Watters, Center for New England Culture, UNH**

*"Julia Older's skill weaving together known history with dramatized human interactions makes one wonder if she might have been living in the 1600s!" —***Cally Gurley, Maine Women Writers Collection**

SUMMARY: In this 17th century novel of Julia Older's Isles of Shoals Trilogy, young Thom Taylor is cast onto the lawless Isles off the New England coast. He falls hopelessly in love with Master Babb's saucy Barbadoes servant Pru. Just when he gains his freedom, Thom is sent on a forced march, survives an Indian massacre, stands trial with a witch, and escapes pirates Quelch and Kidd. Outwitting mutinous sailors hunting for gold, he returns to the Shoals and Pru. Thom's determined struggles bring him independence, prosperity and the family he yearns for as he and adolescent America come of age.

ABOUT THE AUTHOR: **Julia Older** is the author of 25 books. *This Desired Place: The Isles of Shoals* received the 2007 Gold Medal for Best Northeast Regional Fiction from Independent Publisher Book Awards. She edited *Celia Thaxter: Selected Writings* as a companion to her first novel *The Island Queen*. She writes fulltime in New Hampshire.

1. Is this New World saga different from what you learned in school about Colonial Pilgrims? Do the events, laws and customs clash with textbook and popular views of our Founding Fathers and Mothers?

2. The first Shoals novel *The Island Queen* is based on the documented life of writer Celia Thaxter whereas the hero of *This Desired Place* is fictional. Why do you think the author built this deeply researched novel on a fictional character instead of an historical celebrity? How do characteristics of the Shoals shape the characters of the story?

3. Thom pines for a wealthy Major's daughter, Chief's squaw, and Barbadoes servant. What attracts him to such disparate women? If Pru and Thom were in a dating service and saw each other's bios, would being indentured orphans be a turn-on, turn-off or ignored?

4. By chance, Thom and Pru meet Governor Cutt and are married; Will Babb marries a naked woman in an armoire. Describe weddings you attended that were as startling.

5. Why did Goody Cole live in a hovel after she was released from jail? Cite gender discrimination in the novel and discuss housing lending practices faced by 21st century women.

6. Early Shoalers kept records until Phillip Babb's death. What events possibly caused the mysterious halt of record-keeping? Does your town keep historical records? What information is recorded and where is it stored? Are family stories a reliable source of ancestral heritage? What cutting edge technology is used to verify racial-ethnic origins and blood relatives?

7. Of the many children Thom's friend Judge Sewall fathers, only two survive. Yet Sewall was long-lived. Statistics indicate a rise in U.S. infant mortality rates. Are life expectancy and infant mortality reliable indicators of a healthy society? What factors (then and now) have contributed to an increase in adult and infant deaths?

8. Pru collects herbs and dispenses remedies to Thom and other Shoalers. Compare a few of her cures for wounds, colds and menstrual cramps to modern treatments for these ailments.

9. Although Thom isn't a Harvard student, he knows Latin and teaches Shoalers to write their names and keep fishing accounts. How does Thom profit and come up in the New World because of his reading and writing skills?

10. Do these hardscrabble men and women heighten an awareness of your ancestors and their desires for prosperity and freedom?

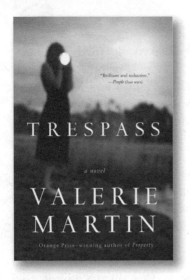

TRESPASS

AUTHOR: *Valerie Martin*

PUBLISHER: Vintage Books, September 2008

WEBSITE: www.ReadingGroupCenter.com

AVAILABLE IN:
Trade Paperback, 304 pages, $14.95
ISBN: 978-1-4000-9551-3

SUBJECT: Family/Culture & World Issues/ Relationships (Fiction)

"Martin is an uncompromising, serious writer, concerned with both the eternal verities and what matters right now. . . . [Trespass] is the best kind of moral fiction, the kind that interrogates morality itself." —New York Times Book Review

SUMMARY: *Trespass* is an ambitious intellectual thriller about a comfortable, cultivated American family forced into sudden proximity with the discomfiting, the lawless, and the wild—particularly the wildness of history.

Chloe Dale's life is in good order. Her only child, Toby, has started his junior year at New York University; her husband, an academic on sabbatical, is working at home on his book about the Crusades; and Chloe is busy creating illustrations for a special edition of Emily Brontë's *Wuthering Heights*. Yet Chloe is disturbed—by the aggression of her government's foreign policy, by the poacher who roams the land behind her studio punctuating her solitude with rifle fire, and finally, by Toby's new girlfriend, a Croatian refugee named Salome Drago.

Chloe distrusts Salome on sight, alienating her from her tolerant husband and besotted son. In shimmering prose Valerie Martin raises the question: who shall inherit America?

ABOUT THE AUTHOR: **Valerie Martin** is the author of three collections of short fiction, most recently *The Unfinished Novel and Other Stories*, and seven novels, including *Italian Fever*, *The Great Divorce*, *Mary Reilly*, the Dr. Jekyll and Mr. Hyde story told from the viewpoint of a housemaid, which was filmed with Julia Roberts and John Malkovich, and the 2003 Orange Prize-winning *Property*. She resides in upstate New York.

CONVERSATION STARTERS

1. What is Chloe's initial impression of Salome? What about her does she find so threatening? Are these the same traits that make her attractive to Toby (and, incidentally, to Brendan)? Are Chloe's perceptions accurate? What clues does the author plant to suggest that she may not be entirely reliable? Conversely, about what does she turn out to be a more accurate judge—and not just of Salome's character?

2. Early on, Toby tries to reassure his mother by telling her that Salome is "very serious." Is he right? What are the possible reasons for Salome's seriousness, and in what ways might those reasons contribute to both her allure and her destructiveness? One synonym for seriousness is gravity. Have the events in Salome's past given her more gravity than the other young women Toby has known? What other characters in the book possess a similar gravity, and what lies behind it?

3. Salome has her own opinions about Chloe. The older woman's seemingly offhand remark about political arguments strikes her as a deliberate insult; her protectiveness of Toby translates as contempt for him. Might any of Salome's perceptions be correct, or do they stem from the same paranoid and totalizing world view that makes her accuse Toby of siding against her and later causes her to turn violently against her father? What other characters in the novel see the world in similar terms, and with what results?

4. Chloe doesn't come to fear and dislike Salome; she feels that way about her from the first, so that even the girl's gaze makes her think of "a spider darting out crazily from some black recess in the basement." The poacher, too, inspires her immediate foreboding and antipathy. Putting aside the question of whether her fears are justified, might they be self-fulfilling? Might Brendan be right when he later observes that "Chloe is making herself sick"? Where else in the novel do people's fears and suspicions become self-fulfilling?

5. In an exchange with Toby's parents, Salome dismisses her family's Cajun neighbors as ignorant. It's one of the few times in the novel when the characters are united in laughter. But the Dales, too, are sometimes ignorant. Chloe wonders if Croats are Muslims and mistakes the poacher for a Middle Easterner. Even characters who are better acquainted with the facts often misinterpret them, as Toby does when he thinks that his bride has left him for MacAlister instead of her mother. Discuss the role that ignorance and misinterpretation play in *Trespass*.

For the complete Reading Group Guide, visit ReadingGroupCenter.com.

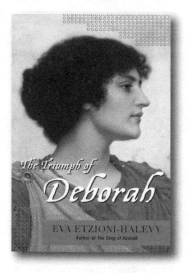

THE TRIUMPH OF DEBORAH

AUTHOR: *Eva Etzioni-Halevy*

PUBLISHER: Plume Books, March 2008

WEBSITE: www.plumebooks.com
www.evaetzionihalevy.com

AVAILABLE IN:
Trade Paperback, 368 pages, $14.00
ISBN: 978-0-452-28906-2

SUBJECT: History/Women's Lives/Faith
(Fiction)

"This novel will be devoured by lovers of historical fiction and romance alike."—Library Journal

SUMMARY: In ancient Israel, war is looming. Deborah, a highly respected leader, has coerced the warrior Barak into launching a strike against the neighboring Canaanites. Against all odds he succeeds, returning triumphantly with Asherah and Nogah, daughters of the Canaanite King, as his prisoners. But military victory is only the beginning of the turmoil, as a complex love triangle develops between Barak and the two princesses.

Deborah, recently cast off by her husband, develops a surprising affinity for Barak. Yet she struggles to rebuild her existence on her own terms, while also groping her way toward the greatest triumph of her life.

A romantic, masterfully written piece of fiction, *The Triumph of Deborah* celebrates the wisdom and the superior guidance of one of the Bible's most powerful and wise women, while also exploring the complex nature of loyalty: to one's nation, to one's family, and to one's own sense of self.

ABOUT THE AUTHOR: **Eva Etzioni-Halevy** is professor emeritus of political sociology at Bar-Ilan University in Israel. She has published fourteen academic books and numerous articles, as well as two previous biblical novels. Eva lives in Tel Aviv with her husband; she has three grown children.

1. Of Deborah, Asherah, or Nogah; whose story did you personally find most compelling? With which woman did you sympathize the most, and with whom did you sympathize the least?
2. Was Lapidoth's divorcement of Deborah as surprising to the reader as it was to Deborah?
3. When Deborah not only agrees to consider Barak's terms, but willingly fulfills those terms upon his return from battling the Canaanites, how does her character change? Is she wiser or more foolish for her affair with Barak? Consider how this particular experience affected her ability to judge people fair and objectively.
4. How very different would the story have been if Sisra had died in a more expected manner?
5. Discuss how Nogah's knowledge and respect for both people make her a key player in the conflict between the two nations.
6. How do we see Barak change over the course of the novel? Is he a likeable character? Is he as compelling to the reader as he is to Deborah and Nogah?
7. Discuss how Asherah's allegiance to her Canaanite background is both her saving grace and her undoing. Compare her devotion to her homeland to Nogah's devotion to Israel and its people.
8. Nogah's trip to see Deborah, and then to leave the scroll she has created with Gilad in the house of the Lord in Shiloh, marks a transformation in the young woman's life. Discuss the extent of her accomplishment: obtaining Deborah's version of the tale, plus the Song of Deborah, and gaining Deborah's approval; then traveling to Shiloh and convincing the elders to house the scroll there. What does this do for Nogah's sense of self and how others view her? How does she change as a result of the trip?
9. Describe the trajectory of the relationship between Nogah and Barak, and how both characters became better people for their interaction with one another. What was Barak forced to realize and accept? What did Nogah teach him? What did Nogah learn about the desires of the human heart—similar to what Deborah learned through her separation from Lapidoth?
10. Consider the final meeting of the Canaanites and the Israelites under Mishma's roof. What does this scene tell us about what has been gained and what has been lost by both nations?
11. How realistic is Etzioni-Halevy's portrayal of ancient Israel? Does this story feel true to its biblical roots? What makes these characters from an ancient time relevant to twenty-first-century readers? What common struggles do we share?

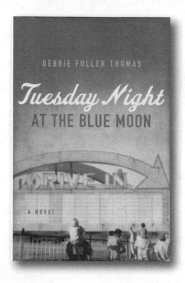

TUESDAY NIGHT
AT THE BLUE MOON

AUTHOR: *Debbie Fuller Thomas*

PUBLISHER: Moody Publishers, June 2008

WEBSITE: www.moodypublishers.com
www.debbiefullerthomas.com

AVAILABLE IN:
Trade Paperback, 368 pages, $13.99
ISBN: 978-0-8024-8733-9

SUBJECT: Family/Faith/Social Issues
(Fiction)

"An unusual plotline and top-notch prose mark this talented novelist's debut . . . competent dialogue, touches of humor, and sparkling character dynamics make this a welcome addition to the faith fiction fold."
—**Publishers Weekly**

SUMMARY: In *Tuesday Night at the Blue Moon*, Debbie Fuller Thomas presents a story of loss and restoration when a family experiences the death of a child, only to discover that she was switched at birth.

Marty is a divorced mother of three struggling to make ends meet by helping her dad operate the Blue Moon Drive-In Theater. After the loss of her daughter, Ginger, to Niemann-Pick (a devastating genetic disease), she discovers the awful truth that Ginger was switched at birth. She receives custody of Andie, her orphaned biological daughter, who refuses to unpack and is adamant that her grandparents will get her back. Marty and Andie each tell their own story, chronicling the journey of a mother and daughter toward acceptance and wholeness, while each struggles in her relationship with how God could let this happen. Will Tuesday night ever be family night again at the Blue Moon?

ABOUT THE AUTHOR: **Debbie Fuller Thomas** has contributed to several story collections. She recently celebrated her ten-year mark as a breast cancer survivor. Debbie and her husband have two adult children and enjoy life in a historic gold rush town in Northern California. *Tuesday Night at the Blue Moon* is her first novel.

1. How does Andie's physical description of the Blue Moon Drive-in reflect the spiritual lives of Marty and Andie as the story begins

2. Marty says the drive-in is "family friendly"? Do you find this ironic, and why or why not? What are the comparisons between the future of drive-in theaters and the traditional family unit?

3. Marty seems eager to "replace" Ginger but Andie isn't eager to "replace" her parents with Marty. What is the difference? In what ways does Marty make Andie feel that she wants her to replace Ginger?

4. Why was it so important to Marty to open a bakery? What does it represent to her, and how does it compare to her father's desire to be an artist? What do Coconut Dandies represent to Winnie, and how does Marty's baking contribute to her need for constant grazing?

5. How would you rate Marty's parenting skills with respect to Deja? Compare it to the relationship between her father and her brother. How do you think Deja will ultimately turn out, and what will she be doing after high school (assuming she graduates)?

6. Marty has a mini-breakdown and ends up many miles from home. Contrast the reasons she left with the reasons she went back. What was the outcome? Did anything change for Marty?

7. At one point, Andie says her "heart-shape is plugged." What specific instances help to loosen the debris inside of Andie in regard to both the family and to God? In what ways is Marty's heart-shape plugged?

8. After several years, Marty is still mourning her broken marriage. At what point does she begin to feel the need for closure?

9. When Marty "dropped" the cake at Julian's feet at the farmer's market, would you say it was more accident or more subconsciously intentional? Who or what did he represent to her at that moment?

10. In what ways does Andie gradually accept that she is really part of the family? On what points does she feel a kinship with Ginger?

11. When Marty finds Ginger's hospital bracelet, she reflects that we are all switched at birth and that God wants to reclaim us. What do you think she means? What would have eventually happened to Andie if Marty hadn't "claimed'" her?

TWENTY WISHES

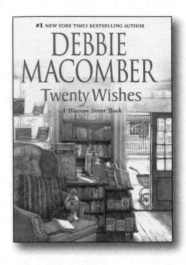

AUTHOR: *Debbie Macomber*

PUBLISHER: Harlequin Enterprises Ltd, May 2008

WEBSITE: www.eHarlequin.com
www.eBooks.eHarlequin.com

AVAILABLE IN:
Hardcover, 360 pages, $24.95
ISBN: 978-0-7783-2550-5

ALSO AVAILABLE IN:
eBook, 360 pages, $22.95
ISBN: 978-1-4268-1610-9

SUBJECT: Family/Relationships/Personal Challenges (Fiction)

"Assured storytelling . . . affirming narrative . . . as welcoming as your favorite easy chair." —**Publishers Weekly**

"Even the most hard-hearted readers will find themselves rooting for the women in this hopeful story while surreptitiously wiping away tears and making their own list of wishes." —**Booklist**

SUMMARY: Anne Marie Roche wants to find happiness again. At thirty-eight, her life's not what she'd expected—she's childless, a recent widow, alone. She owns a successful bookstore on Seattle's Blossom Street, but despite her accomplishments, there's a feeling of emptiness.

On Valentine's Day, Anne Marie and several other widows get together to celebrate . . . what? Hope, possibility, the future. They each begin a list of twenty wishes, things they always wanted to do but never did. Anne Marie's list starts with: Find one good thing about life. She begins to act on her wishes, and when she volunteers at a local school, an eight-year-old girl named Ellen enters her life. It's a relationship that becomes far more involving than Anne Marie intended. It also becomes far more important than she ever imagined.

As Ellen helps Anne Marie complete her list of twenty wishes, they both learn that wishes can come true—but not necessarily in the way you expect.

ABOUT THE AUTHOR: **Debbie Macomber** is one of today's leading voices in women's fiction. A regular on every major bestseller list with more than 100 million copies of her books in print, the award-winning author celebrated a new career milestone in September 2007, when *74 Seaside Avenue* scored #1 on the *New York Times, USA Today, Publishers Weekly* and *Bookscan* bestseller lists.

1. Have you ever written a list of wishes for yourself? How many? Anne Marie Roche and the other widows believe that writing down what you want helps you clarify it—and achieve it. Based on your own experience do you agree? If so, why do you feel that writing down a wish can lead to its fulfillment? What do you think of choosing a number of wishes (as Anne Marie and her friends do), rather than just writing down whatever comes to mind?

2. Anne Marie had agreed to no children before she married Robert, then decided she wanted a baby. What do you think of her actions—and Robert's? Could they have handled things in a better way? What would you have advised them to do? Did you sympathize with her feelings? And did you understand his reasons for not wanting a second family? Did you feel either or both of them acted in a manipulative way?

3. Despite wanting a child in her life and wanting to "do something for someone else," Anne Marie is initially reluctant to get involved with the Lunch Buddy program. Why do you think this is? Inertia? Fear? A sense of inadequacy? Some other reason? What is the primary factor, in your view, that compels her to follow through?

4. Lillie is in many ways a conventional society matron. What gives her the courage to break out of her restricted, although privileged life? Do you think wealth and privilege typically lead to more restrictive attitudes? Realistically, do she and Hector have a chance at a successful relationship?

5. In what ways is Barbie different from her mother? In what ways is she similar? Why is she so attracted to Mark Bassett? Does he represent a challenge to her? Is she drawn to him despite his resistance—or because of it? Where do you see their romance going?

6. The relationship between Anne Marie and her stepdaughter, Melissa, undergoes a profound transformation. What exactly brought it about, in your opinion? Do you understand why the two of them had never been able to connect, considering that Melissa was 13 at the time Anne Marie married Robert? Who's to blame for this—or is it even a question of blame? If you were Anne Marie, would you have done anything differently?

7. By the end of the story, Anne Marie finds what she was missing in life. And she finds it in unexpected ways. Did her list of 20 Wishes contribute to making this possible? If so, how? Have you made wishes that were fulfilled in ways you did not expect?"

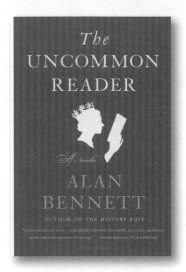

THE UNCOMMON READER

AUTHOR: *Alan Bennett*

PUBLISHER: Picador, October 2008

WEBSITE: www.picadorusa.com

AVAILABLE IN:
Trade Paperback, 128 pages, $12.00
ISBN: 978-0-312-42764-1

SUBJECT: Culture & World Issues/ Humor/ Family (Fiction)

"One of the greatest living English writers." —**David Thomson,** *The Nation*

"Bennett's deadpan, self-deprecating humor translates perfectly." —**David Gates,** *O, The Oprah Magazine*

"There is probably no other distinguished English man of letters more instantly likable than Bennett." —**Michael Dirda,** *The Washington Post Book World*

SUMMARY: By turns cheeky and charming, the novella features the Queen herself as its protagonist. When her yapping corgis lead her to a mobile library, Her Majesty develops a new obsession with reading. She finds herself devouring works by a tantalizing range of authors, from the Brontë sisters to Jean Genet. With a young member of the palace kitchen staff guiding her choices, it's not long before the Queen begins to develop a new perspective on the world—one that alarms her closest advisers and tempts her to make bold new decisions.

ABOUT THE AUTHOR: **Alan Bennett** has been one of England's leading dramatists since the success of *Beyond the Fringe*. His work includes the *Talking Heads* television series and the stage plays *Forty Years On, The Lady in the Van, A Question of Attribution*, and *The Madness of George III*. His debut novella, *The Clothes They Stood Up In*, was a *Today Show* Book Club Pick. His most recent play, *The History Boys*, won six Tony Awards, including Best Play. It was also released as a feature film. His memoir, *Untold Stories,* was a #1 bestseller in the U.K. and he was named the Author of the Year at the 2006 British Book Awards.

1. Does your group meet regularly? If so, how do you think the Queen, as fountain of honor, would appraise your list of reading so far?

2. The Queen says that she reads because, "One has a duty to find out what people are like." Yet she begins by reading Nancy Mitford and Ivy Compton-Burnett, hardly a stretch for Her Royal Majesty. How did you begin your reading career? Was it *Anne of Green Gables* or Barbara Cartland? What treasured books on your group's list closely reflect your own world and background? Do you read to understand others? Is anyone present at this meeting a member of the titled aristocracy?

3. Do you believe there is a difference between reading and experiencing? Isn't the act of reading a form of experience, or is that vein of thinking distinctly privileged?

4. At first the Queen says that her purpose in reading is not primarily literary: it is for analysis and reflection. Why exactly do you read; is it a lofty endeavor or a fundamentally human one?

5. What do you think of the Queen's values as a reader, for example her insistence upon reading a book all the way through to the end, regardless of her level of engagement? Surely most of us would put a book down if within fifty pages it proved to be a tedious waste of time. Have you ever attempted to discuss a book you haven't read?

6. Authors, the Queen decides, were probably best met within the pages of their novels, left to the imagination like their characters. Have you met any famous writers? What were they like? Was your experience anything like the Queen's?

7. The appeal of books, according to the Queen, lay in their indifference: there is something undeferring about literature, she says. Books do not care who reads them or whether one read them or not. All readers are equal, herself included. Do you agree? Have you ever felt unequal to a book? Superior to one?

8. When the Queen begins to ask her subjects what they are reading, she is usually met with a shrug (or the Bible, or *Harry Potter*). Are people intimidated by reading, or are they just lazy and dim?

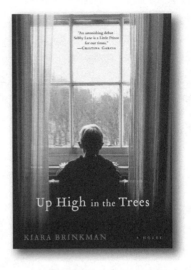

UP HIGH IN THE TREES

AUTHOR: *Kiara Brinkman*

PUBLISHER: Grove Press, June 2008

WEBSITE: www.grovepress.com

AVAILABLE IN:
Trade Paperback, 352 pages, $14.00
ISBN: 978-0-8021-4370-9

SUBJECT: Family/Coming of Age/
Personal Discovery (Fiction)

A Book Sense Selection
A Borders Original Voices Selection
A Barnes & Noble Discover Selection
Chicago Tribune Favorite Books of 2007

"The treasures here are exquisite. . . . This is a heartbreaking novel, which should be read in a single, reverent hush. . . . Sebby's innocent voice speaks for anyone bravely grasping for order and solace amid unspeakable loss." —**Ron Charles, *The Washington Post***

SUMMARY: All who know young Sebby Lane understand that he is an unusual child in many respects—that he experiences the world around him more vividly than most, a condition that only intensifies after the death of his best friend: his mother. Sebby misses her so acutely that he begins to dream and even relive moments of her life. When Sebby's father decides to take Sebby to live in the family's summerhouse, he hopes it will give them both the time and space they need to recover. But Sebby's father deteriorates in this new isolation, leaving Sebby to come to terms with his mother's death alone as he wonders if he, too, is meant to share her fate.

In spare and fierce prose buoyed by the life force of its small, fearless narrator, *Up High in the Trees* introduces an astonishingly fresh and powerful literary voice.

ABOUT THE AUTHOR: **Kiara Brinkman** graduated from Brown University and recently earned her M.F.A. in writing from Goddard College in Vermont. She lives in San Francisco.

1. How would you describe the voice of Sebby, the narrator? Does he seem troubled, perhaps as a result of the early loss of his mother, or something else? Does his voice sound erratic and unstable to you, or is he particularly alert and sensitive?

2. Why do you suppose the setting is left vague? Is it perhaps to leave the story as a kind of fable, with truths for all times? Might the compression of the action in one year, with flashbacks, add to this mythic quality?

3. What do we know about the interior lives of characters other than Sebby? We can deduce attitudes and feelings, but it is all through what filter? Why might that be?

4. How is food important for sustaining family life or marking occasions? Is it telling that the story ends with a feast?

5. What is the function of Sebby's letter writing to his teacher? How did you respond to those letters? Do the letters offer an important counter-point to the rest of the narration?

6. At one point Dad says, "We still have to be a family." Even though the mother is said to have "left," how does she provide an enduring legacy?

7. What are some of the precarious mental states in the book? Is there a symbolic connection between hiding under tables and beds and wandering out into the night?

8. How do pictures provide both a solace and a hope for the future for Sebby?

9. Are you familiar with the songs that provide a framework of memory for the father—and by extension for his children? Is music actually one of the ways they become a family?

10. How are books central to the lives of these children? Do you think that Sebby's love of reading reassures the social worker? What is the father's connection with books?

11. What does the title mean? Could it imply something about Sebby's special vantage point in the story?

12. Talk about Sebby's view of time in the tale. When does he want to accelerate it? Slow it down? Retrieve lost time? How does the dark hiding place at the end change from earlier hiding places? How has Sebby's idea of time evolved?

13. Even though the book often focuses on loss, specific as well as ele-mental, how is it also about restoration and redemption? How do love and patience, loyalty and courage work their magic?

14. What do you predict for the family in the future?

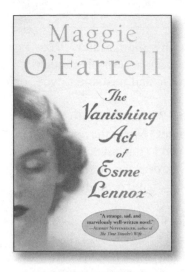

THE VANISHING ACT OF ESME LENNOX

AUTHOR: Maggie O'Farrell

PUBLISHER: Houghton Mifflin Harcourt
June 2008

WEBSITE: www.maggieofarrell.com

AVAILABLE IN:
Paperback, 256 pages, $14.00
ISBN: 9780156033671

Subject: Relationships/Family/Identity
(Fiction)

"The novel is brilliant in every way. With devastating clarity, O'Farrell shows the dangerous webs through which people conspire to present an acceptable front and how, years later, when the initial protagonists are dead and history seems set, another story can emerge to confound everything. . . . Maggie O'Farrell has written a taut, fragile mystery of relationships and deception." —**Literary Review**

"Deliciously paced, classic O'Farrell." —**Good Housekeeping**

SUMMARY: In the middle of tending to the everyday business at her vintage-clothing shop and sidestepping her married boyfriend's attempts at commitment, Iris Lockhart receives a stunning phone call: Her great-aunt Esme, whom she never knew existed, is being released from Cauldstone Hospital—where she has been locked away for more than sixty-one years. Iris's grandmother Kitty always claimed to be an only child. But Esme's papers prove she is Kitty's sister, and Iris can see the shadow of her dead father in Esme's face. If Iris takes her in, what dangerous truths might she inherit? A gothic, intricate tale of family secrets, lost lives, and the freedom brought by truth, *The Vanishing Act of Esme Lennox* will haunt you long past its final page.

ABOUT THE AUTHOR: **Maggie O'Farrell** was born in Northern Ireland in 1972, and grew up in Wales and Scotland. She now lives in Edinburgh with her family. Her debut novel, *After You'd Gone*, was published to international acclaim, and won a Betty Trask Award, while her third, *The Distance Between Us*, won the 2005 Somerset Maugham Award.

1. When Iris gets the call from the psychiatric hospital, she is put in a very difficult position. What does she stand to gain and lose from the decision she eventually makes? What would you do in her shoes?

2. How have years of incarceration affected Esme? Has she retained any of the qualities we see in young Esme, before she is committed? Does she seem sane to you?

3. The story contains several twists—what are they, and which did you find the most shocking?

4. Considering all that Kitty has done, all that has happened to her, and the dementia she has suffered in old age, are you able to feel sympathetic towards her?

5. The relationship between Iris and Alex is a complex one. How does it seem to have influenced their relationships with others? By the end of the novel, do you think they had reached any kind of resolution?

6. How did you find the end of the book? Can you think of any alternative endings that might have worked?

7. What similarities, and what differences do you see between the younger Esme, and the younger Iris?

8. This is a novel with a very complex time scheme. What techniques does the author use to handle this?

9. This has been described as Maggie O'Farrell's best novel so far. Do you agree?

10. The relationship between the sisters is very complicated. In what ways does it change as they enter adulthood?

11. How do you think people's attitudes towards unmarried mothers have changed since Esme was a young girl? How different would her life have been had she been able to keep her baby?

12. What do you feel the book tells us about mental institutions? Do you think people's attitudes have changed since the first half of the 20th century?

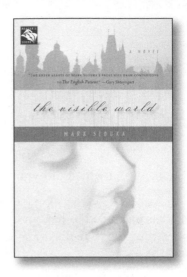

THE VISIBLE WORLD

AUTHOR: *Mark Slouka*

PUBLISHER: Mariner Books, March 2008

WEBSITE: www.marinerbooks.com

AVAILABLE IN:
Trade Paperback, 256 pages, $13.95
ISBN: 978-0-547-05367-7

SUBJECT: Family/History/Love (Fiction)

"Rich with intelligence and poetic detail, The Visible World *demonstrates why Mark Slouka is one of our finest contemporary novelists. He makes us think; he makes us feel; and because what he does is not just storytelling but art, we are elevated in the reading of his work."*
—**Elizabeth Berg, author of** *We Are All Welcome Here*

SUMMARY: An immensely moving, powerfully romantic novel about the vagaries of love and the legacy of war, *The Visible World* is narrated by the American-born son of Czech immigrants. His New York childhood, lived in a boisterous community of the displaced, is suffused with stories: fragments of European history, Czech fairy tales, and family secrets gleaned from overheard conversations. Central in his young imagination is the heroic account of the seven Czech parachutists who, in 1942, assassinated a high-ranking Nazi. Yet one essential story has always evaded him: his mother's. He suspects she had a great wartime love, the loss of which bred a sadness that slowly engulfed her. As an adult, the narrator travels to Prague, hoping to piece together her hidden past.

ABOUT THE AUTHOR: **Mark Slouka** is the author of the novel *God's Fool,* named a Best Book of the Year by the *San Francisco Chronicle*, the short story collection *Lost Lake*, a *New York Times* Notable Book in 1998, and the nonfiction work *War of the Worlds*. He is a contributing editor at *Harper's Magazine* and is currently the director of the writing program at the University of Chicago.

1. *The Visible World* is divided into three sections—each of which represents a different approach to the same essential story. Which section, do you think, is most "true"? Why? How do the three sections play off of each other to create a complex whole?

2. What haunts the narrator's family, his community? How do the ghosts of the past shape the course of the narrator's life?

3. Do you believe that the narrator is ultimately able to reassemble a version of history that closely resembles the true events? How so or how not? Why does he try so earnestly to piece together the story?

4. How would you characterize the relationship between the narrator's parents, Antonín and Ivana, as portrayed in "The New World: A Memoir"?

5. What compels us to construct stories out of our own histories? How does *The Visible World* illustrate this need?

6. How does *The Visible World* investigate the profound impact of secrecy, of information withheld, in love and in war? How are the lives of its characters shaped by what is known and what is unknown?

7. Who suffered most as a result of their love? Who lost the most? Would you describe theirs as a "good love story"? Why or why not?

8. When streets in Prague's Old Town were inundated by floodwaters, first floors became cellars. In what way does this physical world buried beneath the present world work as metaphor? How does it relate to the novel's title, *The Visible World?*

9. How do you suppose the passage of time has altered the characters' memories of life in prewar and wartime Europe?

10. What factors initially draw Tomáš and Ivana together? Do you believe the relationship would have lasted if it were not for the events of war? Why or why not?

11. Tomáš and Ivana's love affair takes place in a setting seemingly far removed from the bleak realities of wartime. What does the near-mythical forest represent in the context of the novel?

12. The epigraph of *The Visible World* is taken from the poem "As I Walked Out One Evening" by W. H. Auden. How do Auden's lines resonate in Slouka's novel?

13. The novel opens and ends with the same scene, that of Antonín getting dressed in the dark to go out and search for Ivana, who had gone for a walk in the forest at night. How does the context provided by the novel change how you perceive this scene? What emotions does it stir with each telling?

WHEN THE WHITE HOUSE WAS OURS

AUTHOR: *Porter Shreve*

PUBLISHER: Mariner Books, Fall 2008

WEBSITE: www.portershreve.com
www.marinerbooks.com

AVAILABLE IN:
Paperback, 288 pages, $12.95
ISBN: 978-0-618-72210-5

SUBJECT: Family/Relationships/
American History (Fiction)

"When the White House Was Ours *is as good as it gets. Porter Shreve tells the story of the Truitts, a most unusual displaced family who come to Washington, DC from the Midwest to start an alternative school in a white house. They arrive about the same time Jimmy Carter, the man from Plains, comes to another White House with a credo about trust. The end result is a tale of sheer delight.*" —**Jim Lehrer, Host of "The NewsHour with Jim Lehrer" and author of** *Eureka* **and** *The Last Debate*

It's 1976 and while the country prepares to celebrate the bicentennial Daniel's family is falling apart. His father, Pete, has been fired from yet another teaching job, and his mother, Valerie, is one step away from packing up the van and leaving for good. But when Pete convinces a wealthy old friend and rival to lend him a crumbling mansion in Washington, D.C., mere blocks from the White House, he makes a bold plan: to move east and start a democratic school under his own roof, where students and teachers are equals. *When the White House Was Ours* is a story about a family's struggle to stay together and pursue a dream against all odds, and a nostalgic reflection on a time when the White House was in the hands, however briefly, of idealists.

ABOUT THE AUTHOR: **Porter Shreve** is the author of *The Obituary Writer,* which was a finalist for the Great Lakes Booksellers Award and for the Society of Midland Authors Book of the Year. It was also a *New York Times* Notable Book. He is also the author of *Drives Like Dream,* which was a *Chicago Tribune* Book Best of the Year selection. Shreve an associate professor at Purdue University. He divides his time between West Lafayette, Indiana, and Chicago, Illinois, and is married to the writer Bich Minh Nguyen.

1. The narrator of *When the White House Was Ours* is a 12-year-old boy. What makes Daniel a good choice to tell the story?

2. How are the adult Daniel and the 12-year-old Daniel similar or different? Why is Daniel's experience at Our House still so important to him, nearly twenty-five years later?

3. For the first several months after his family arrives in Washington, Daniel plays the role of his father's right hand man. Why is he so eager to please and protect his father?

4. The arrival of the hippies Tino, Cinnamon and Linc marks a turning point in the story. To what extent do they help or hurt the cause of the school? In what ways are they representative of the successes and failures of the 1960s as a cultural phenomenon?

5. Early in the novel Val tells her husband, "This was your idea" and seems as if she'd rather wait and watch than help bail Pete out of trouble. But soon she becomes active in trying to help the school succeed. What changes in Val?

6. One of the earliest students to enroll in the school had at first been a robbery suspect. What is Quinn's role in the story? In what ways is he similar to certain other characters? What do you make of his obsession with flying machines, both literally and metaphorically?

7. Quinn's entrance is dramatic, but it's not the first scene in which theft is a focal point. What do you make of all the stealing? Did you find yourself rooting for the thieves?

8. In what ways does the presidential history that Daniel collects mirror the goings-on at Our House? What were some of your favorite presidential tidbits?

9. Interpret the title *When the White House Was Ours*. How many White Houses or white houses does the title refer to? To what extent is the novel a story of the 1970s or a story of our own time?

10. On various occasions throughout the novel, Daniel hears "a faint clicking in the walls and a rustling sound" and he begins to worry that the place is haunted. Is the house haunted, either literally or metaphorically? If so, who are the ghosts?

11. In what ways does the Our House democratic experiment succeed and in what ways does it fail? What are the school's plusses and minuses?

12. What do you make of Pete's decision to make an example of Daniel by locking him in jail? How does this act mark a turning point in the story and in Daniel's relationship with his father?

13. After you'd turned the last page, did you feel the novel was funny or sad?

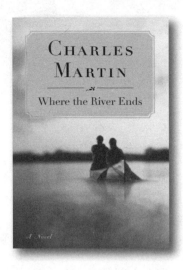

WHERE THE RIVER ENDS

AUTHOR: *Charles Martin*

PUBLISHER: Broadway Books, July 2008

WEBSITE: www.broadwaybooks.com
www.charlesmartinbooks.com

AVAILABLE IN:
Hardcover, 384 pages, $19.95
ISBN: 978-0-7679-2698-0

SUBJECTS: Relationships/Personal
Challenges/Inspiration (Fiction)

"Martin brings to life the varying flora and fauna of this often fraught journey, while he captures the singular atmosphere of life on a changeable river as it traverses through varying Georgian and Floridian terrain. In the tradition of Nicholas Sparks and Robert James Waller, Martin has fashioned a heartbreaking story." ——**Publishers Weekly**

SUMMARY: A powerfully emotional and beautifully written story of heart-breaking loss and undying love.

He was a fishing guide and struggling artist from a south George trailer park. She was the beautiful only child of South Carolina's most powerful senator. Yet once Doss Michaels and Abigail Grace Coleman met by accident, they each felt they'd found their true soul mate.

Ten years into their marriage, when Abbie faces a life-threatening illness, Doss battles it with her every step of the way. And when she makes a list of ten things she hopes to accomplish before she loses the fight for good, Doss is there, too, supporting her and making everything possible. Together they steal away in the middle of the night to embark upon a 130-mile trip down the St. Mary's River—a voyage Doss promised Abbie in the early days of their courtship.

Where the River Ends chronicles their love-filled, tragedy-tinged journey and a bond that transcends all.

ABOUT THE AUTHOR: **Charles Martin** is the author of six novels. He and his family live in Jacksonville, Florida.

1. What does Doss's mother teach him in the novel's opening scenes? What gift does she give him through the words "if you ever find your well empty, nothing but dust—then you come back here … dive in and drink deeply"?

2. Doss recalls overcoming his suffocating asthma and growing up without a father figure. Abbie had to cope with the death of her mother and life with a domineering father. In what ways did Doss and Abbie heal each other through love?

3. Discuss the Saint Mary's River as a character in *Where the River Ends*. What "personality" is reflected in the variety of scenes depicting the river? How does the timeless symbolism of water—as cleansing, life-sustaining, and ever-changing—shape its power in the novel? Where does the river ultimately take Doss and Abbie?

4. What does the novel indicate about modern medicine and its limits? What was Doss able to do for Abbie that no doctor could?

5. Doss's first up-close encounter with Abbie occurs when he fends off her attacker. During their river journey, they must again defend themselves against other threatening characters. What is the nature of such evil in the world? What determines whether victims remain optimistic, like Doss and Abbie, or descend into a quest for vengeance?

6. How does Doss and Abbie's journey down the river compare to their fantasy of it? What does it say about them that, despite the lack of creature comforts or security, they are able to savor every moment of the voyage? Why was Abbie better off without traditional hospice care?

7. Which of the wishes on Abbie's list seemed the most difficult to achieve? Which one would have been the most exhilarating for you?

8. How was the storytelling enhanced by the author's use of flashbacks? In what way did the timeline mirror the way memories are woven into the present?

9. Were you surprised by the scene of forgiveness in the end? What did Doss and his father-in-law ultimately have in common?

10. Describe the most important farewell you have experienced. Have you ever served as the navigator for someone who had to endure a difficult journey?

11. If you were faced with Abbie's prognosis, what unfulfilled promises and unfinished wishes would you make haste to experience? What would it take to accomplish the dreams on this list even if you were not faced with Abbie's fate?

WIFE IN THE NORTH
350 Miles from Home with Three Young Children, Two Aging Parents, and One Absentee Husband

AUTHOR: *Judith O'Reilly*

PUBLISHER: PublicAffairs, August 2008

WEBSITE: www.publicaffairsbooks.com

AVAILABLE IN:
Trade Paperback, 336 pages, $14.95
ISBN: 978-1-58648-639-6

SUBJECT: Women's Lives/Family/Identity
(Memoir)

"Cold Comfort Farm *with booster seats. Funny, honest and moving.*" —**Stephanie Calman author of** *Confessions of a Bad Mother*

"*Genuinely funny and genuinely moving.*"—**Jane Fallon author of** *Getting Rid of Matthew*

SUMMARY: Perhaps it was because she was pregnant and hormones had eaten her brain that Judith O'Reilly was persuaded by her husband to leave London for the northern wilds. But pregnancy hadn't addled her enough not to have a back-up plan: if life in the country didn't measure up, the family would return to the city. Far from home, Judith, a journalist and mother of three young children, discovers just how tough an assignment making a new life is. In the heart of the country, with no decent coffee in sight, Judith swaps high heels for rubber boots and media-darlings for evangelical strangers and farmers' wives, in an effort to do that simple thing that women do—make hers a happy family.

O'Reilly's headlong foray into the country invites adventure at every turn, and offers a hilarious, heartfelt reflection on how to navigate the challenges and rewards of motherhood, marriage, and family, while searching for one's own true north in an alien landscape.

ABOUT THE AUTHOR: **Judith O'Reilly** was the education correspondent for *The Sunday Times of London*, where she also reported on politics and news, and worked undercover on education and social and criminal justice investigations. She is a former political producer for ITV's Channel 4 News and BBC2's Newsnight. A freelance journalist, she started her blog www.wifeinthenorth.com in 2006. She lives in England.

1. Judith concedes to move out of London to accommodate her husband's desire to live in the country, yet he continues to commute to the city to work while she remains at home. At the end of the day, do you consider this a fair trade? Why or why not?

2. "Wifey" is a classic city-mouse in the country. How does her experience in the country change her relationship to the city? How well does she adapt to her new surroundings?

3. As the mother of three young children, and the daughter of aging parents, Judith admits to not knowing whether to run for her four-year-old or to remain with her hesitant mother for fear that she may trip. How does this "damned if you do, damned if you don't" experience motivate Judith? How accurately do you think it represents the experiences of women who have children at a later age?

4. What do you see as Judith O'Reilly's primary concern in life? How do her priorities reflect, or differ, from your own?

5. Does the country make Judith become more of an adult? Why or why not?

6. Late in the book, we learn that Judith's first child was stillborn. How do you think this experience has shaped her relationship to her three children? To her idea of family? Does Judith consider her friends more akin to family than most people?

7. After Judith writes in her blog about her son's experience of being bullied in school, she's ostracized by some members of the school community. What's your understanding of their reaction? Was she out of line to write publicly about the events? Why or why not?

8. Judith sees blogging as a sort of online diary accessible to any and all. Do you agree? How well do you feel you know the author by the end of the book?

9. What are the potential ramifications of blogging about family life?

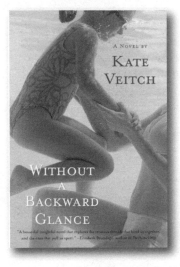

WITHOUT A BACKWARD GLANCE

AUTHOR: *Kate Veitch*

PUBLISHER: Plume Books, June 2008

WEBSITE: www.plumebooks.com
www.kateveitch.com

AVAILABLE IN:
Trade Paperback, 384 pages, $14.00
ISBN: 9-78-0-452-28947-5

SUBJECT: Family/Women's Lives/
Relationships (Fiction)

"Warm and always honest, Veitch manages to capture the ebb and flow of sibling dynamics and illuminate the mixed bag of emotions that comes with family life." —**Vogue** Australia

"Impossible to put down." —**Australian Women's Weekly**

SUMMARY: On a stifling Christmas Eve in 1967, the lives of the McDonald children—Deborah, Robert, James, and Meredith—changed forever. Their mother, Rosemarie, told them she was running out to buy some lights for the tree. She never came back. The children were left with their father, and a gnawing question: why had their mother abandoned them? Over the years, the four siblings have become practiced in concealing their pain, remaining close into adulthood, and forming their own families. But long-closed wounds are reopened when a chance encounter brings James face-to-face with Rosemarie after nearly forty years. Secrets that each sibling has locked away come to light as they struggle to come to terms with their mother's reappearance, while at the same time their beloved father is progressing into dementia. Veitch's family portrait reveals the joys and sorrows, the complexity and ambiguity of family life, and poignantly probes what it means to love and what it means to leave.

ABOUT THE AUTHOR: **Kate Veitch** was born in Adelaide in the mid-1950s and left home and school early. Her work includes writing articles and reviews for the *Sydney Morning Herald* and *Vogue*; collaborating with other mothers on *Feeling Our Way*, a book about becoming parents; and producing a series on women writers, *Their Brilliant Careers*, for Radio National. She lives part-time in Manhattan and part-time in Melbourne. *Without a Backward Glance* is her first novel.

1. About the title, *Without a Backward Glance*—what do you feel is the significance of someone taking "a backward glance": does it represent regret, or reflection, or something else? How important is the title of a novel to you, and what do you think of the Australian title *Listen*?

2. To what extent were the lives and personalities of each of the children shaped by their mother's departure and absence? Do you think they would have had similar personalities and traits if she hadn't gone?

3. Was the situation Rosemarie faced in Australia in 1967 much different from the one she would have faced if she had been living in America? Was the Australian setting an important part of the novel for you?

4. Do you believe perfect parental love exists? If so, what shape does it take?

5. Did you find Rosemarie's abandonment of her family believable? Forgivable? Why do you think a woman leaving her children is still such a taboo?

6. What might Rosemarie's life have been like if she had stayed? What sort of family do you think the McDonalds would, or could, have been?

7. There are many instances of secrecy in *Without a Backward Glance*. Does every family have secrets? What is their role?

8. What value does truth have to the McDonald family? What value does truth have to you?

9. Does Alex's dementia deepen the rifts between the members of his family, or draw them together? How do you think they will cope as it worsens?

10. After James finds his mother, his sexual relationship with his wife, Silver, blossoms. Why was it so lacking before this? And what was it about finding his mother that influenced such a change?

11. Why does Olivia have so few friends her own age? What do you think of this?

12. Would Angus have entered into the affair with Marion if his home circumstances had been different? Who is responsible for this—Angus? Deborah? Marion?

13. Do you think Laurence has been harmed by his mother's alcoholism?

14. Do you believe the characters in *Without a Backward Glance* are held accountable for their faults and misdeeds? If not, how does this make you respond?

Lady Banks' Commonplace Book

a newsletter for people who love Southern Literature (and literary gossip)

Book Reviews from Southern Booksellers

Author Readings & Book Signings

Book Festivals & Literary Events

Literary News & Gossip

Interviews

Essays & Commentary

Excerpts in Excellent Literary Taste

(as selected by Her ladyship, the editor)

subscribe now at ladybanks@sibaweb.com
also available at

authorsroundthesouth.com

Visit the **VP BOOK CLUB**
to enhance your
READING GROUP EXPERIENCE

vpbookclub.com

GREAT CLASSICS

make great reading group choices

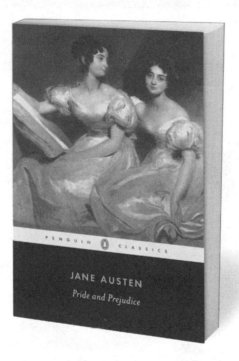

www.penguinclassics.com

www.vpbookclub.com

Penguin Classics
A member of Penguin Group (USA)

Best Bets For Reading Groups:

Stephen L. Carter
New England White
This national bestseller is the electrifying new novel from the author of *The Emperor of Ocean Park*, which returns us to Elm Harbor, where a murder begins to crack the New England university town's polished veneer. BCALA Literary Fiction Winner.
978-0-375-71291-3 | $14.95/$16.95C
Vintage | TR | Available Now

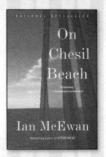

Ian McEwan
On Chesil Beach
In 1962, Florence and Edward celebrate their wedding in a hotel on the Dorset coast. Yet as they dine, the expectation of their marital duties weighs over them. And unbeknownst to both, the decisions they make this night will resonate throughout their lives. An ALA Notable Book.
978-0-307-38617-5 | $13.95
Anchor | TR | Available Now

Tawni O'Dell
Sister Mine: A Novel
Set in the fictional Pennsylvania town of Jolly Mount, *Sister Mine* has all the Tawni O'Dell trademarks: dark humor, tenderness, narrative drive, an effortlessly absorbing female narrator, and a keen sense of place.
978-0-307-35167-8 | $14.95/$16.95C
Three Rivers Press | TR | Available Now

Nicholas Griffin
Dizzy City: A Novel
It's 1916 and Europe is at war. Englishman Benedict Cramb deserts the trench warfare of northern France and stows away on a transatlantic ship. When he arrives in a city untouched by and largely unaware of the horrors of war, he realizes New York is the place to reinvent himself.
978-1-58195-228-5 | $14.95/$16.95C
Steerforth Press | TR | September

Von Hardesty and Gene Eisman
Epic Rivalry: The Inside Story of the Soviet and American Space Race
Following the 50th anniversary of the Sputnik Launch, two noted experts offer a fresh history of the epic race to the moon.
978-1-4262-0321-3 | $16.95/$20.00C
National Geographic | TR | September

Sandra Kring
Thank You for All Things
A powerful and poignant novel by a brilliant storyteller who illustrates that when it comes to matters of family and love, often it is the innocent who force others to confront their darkest secrets.
978-0-385-34120-2 | $12.00/$14.00C
Bantam Discovery | TR | September

Discussible Titles *from* Random House, Inc.

Adalbert Stifter
Rock Crystal
Seemingly the simplest of stories —a passing anecdote of village life—*Rock Crystal* opens up into a tale of almost unendurable suspense that may also be read as a tale of deep spiritual crisis and unlooked-for consolation. Certainly this jewel-like novella is among the most unusual, moving, and memorable of Christmas stories.
978-1-59017-285-8 | $12.95/$14.95C
New York Review Books | TR | September

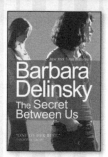

Barbara Delinsky
The Secret Between Us
An unforgettable story about making bad choices for the right reasons and the terrible consequences of a lie gone wrong.
978-0-7679-2519-8 | $14.00/$16.50C
Broadway | TR | October

Tissa Abeysekara
Bringing Tony Home
Part memoir and part fiction, this elegant collection from an award-winning author comprises a novella and three short stories about a historically compelling coming-of-age in Sri Lanka in the 1940's and 1950's.
978-1-55643-757-1 | $14.95/$16.95C
North Atlantic | TR | November

Azar Nafisi
Reading Lolita in Tehran: A Memoir in Books
An expanded deluxe edition of the *New York Times* #1 bestseller. Featuring new material including an updated reading group guide, an exclusive interview with the author, and an excerpt for Nafisi's new memoir.
978-0-8129-7930-5 | $16.00/$19.00C
RH Trade Paperbacks | TR | November

James Runcie
Canvey Island: A Novel
Profoundly moving and elegantly written, *Canvey Island* tells the story of changing times In post-war Britain through one family's tragedy and loss.
Reading Group Guide available.
Visit: www.otherpress.com
978-1-59051-293-7 | $13.95/NCR
Other Press | TR Original | November

RANDOM HOUSE, INC.

Visit us at:
www.randomhouse.com
/library
to Sign Up for our
Monthly e-Newsletter
Bookgroups@Random

Visit
www.randomhouse.com/rgg
to browse hundreds of
Reading Group Guides

JOIN THE CIRCLE

Register your book club and receive a free copy of our *Book Club Companion* quarterly magazine—the perfect tool to find out about current releases and to help reading groups pick the right book.

Once you have signed up, you will also be eligible to occasionally receive free copies of our latest Random House Reader's Circle books and to share your thoughts with us! Feedback is encouraged and rewarded—if we hear from you about books we have sent, you will become part of our "Inner Circle" and we'll be happy to send you more books!

TESTIMONIALS FROM BOOK CLUB MEMBERS

"Thank you very much for the quarterly *Companion*. It was a wonderful surprise to find it in my mailbox. The book suggestions are wonderful not only for my book group but also for individual reading selections. I hope to receive more new [magazine] releases in the mail, I had no idea that I would be receiving these when I signed up, thank you!"
—STEPHANIE SPANGLER, The Book Babes

"I love it! Not only did I add a few books to my 'must-read' list, but I enjoyed reviewing ones that I have already read. I will be sure to share this with all my book club members next week!"
—JULIE PETERSON, Preschool Moms Book Club

JOIN THE CIRCLE TODAY!
Visit www.randomhousereaderscircle.com
to receive your FREE book club magazine
The Random House Publishing Group

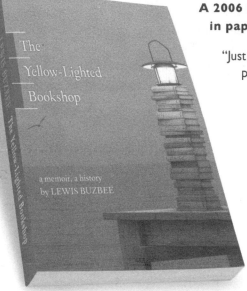

READING GROUP Choices

We wish to thank the authors, agents, publicists, librarians, booksellers, and our publishing colleagues who have continued to support this publication by calling to our attention some quality books for group discussion, and the publishers and friends who have helped to underwrite this edition.

Algonquin Books of Chapel Hill	Mariner Books
Appledore Books	Moody Publishers
Atlantic Monthly Press	Penguin Books
Avon A	Picador USA
Ballantine Books	Plume
Broadway Books	PublicAffairs
Conari Press	Random House
Doubleday Books	Simon Spotlight Entertainment
Europa Editions	Soho Press
Forge	Southern Independent Booksellers Alliance
Free Press	
Graywolf Press	Thomas Dunne Books
Grove Press	Tor
Harlequin Enterprise, Ltd.	Unbridled Books
Harper Paperbacks	Vanguard Press
Harper Perennial	Vintage Books
Houghton Mifflin Harcourt	Voice
Hyperion	William Morrow

Reading Group Choices' goal is to join with publishers, bookstores, libraries, trade associations, and authors to develop resources to enhance the reading group experience.

Reading Group Choices is distributed annually to bookstores, libraries, and directly to book groups. Titles from previous issues are posted on the **www.ReadingGroupChoices.com** website. Books presented here have been recommended by book group members, librarians, booksellers, literary agents, publicists, authors, and publishers. All submissions are then reviewed to ensure the discussibility of each title. Once a title is approved for inclusion by the Advisory Board (see below), publishers are asked to underwrite production costs, so that copies of *Reading Group Choices* can be distributed for a minimal charge.

For additional copies, please call your local library or bookstore, or contact us by phone or email as shown below. Quantities are limited. For more information, please visit our website at **www.ReadingGroupChoices.com**

Toll-free: 1-866-643-6883 • info@ReadingGroupChoices.com

READING GROUP CHOICES' ADVISORY BOARD

Donna Paz Kaufman founded the bookstore training and consulting group of Paz & Associates in 1992, with the objective of creating products and services to help independent bookstores and public libraries remain viable in today's market. A few years later, she met and married **Mark Kaufman**, whose background included project management, marketing communications, and human resources. Together, they launched **Reading Group Choices** in 1994 to bring publishers, booksellers, libraries, and readers closer together. They sold **Reading Group Choices** to Barbara and Charlie Mead in May 2005. They now offer training and education for new and prospective booksellers, architectural design services for bookstores and libraries, marketing support through *The Reader's Edge* customer newsletter, and some print and video products on a wide variety of topics. To learn more about Paz & Associates, visit www.pazbookbiz.com.

John Mutter is editor-in-chief of *Shelf Awareness*, the daily e-mail newsletter focusing on books, media about books, retailing and related issues to help booksellers, librarians and others do their jobs more effectively.

Before he and his business partner, Jenn Risko, founded the company in May 2005, he was executive editor of bookselling at *Publishers Weekly*. He has covered book industry issues for 25 years and written for a variety of publications, including *The Bookseller* in the U.K.; *Australian Bookseller & Publisher*; *Boersenblatt*, the German book trade magazine; and *College Store Magazine* in the U.S. For more information about *Shelf Awareness*, go to its Web site, www.shelf-awareness.com.

Mark Nichols was an independent bookseller in various locations from Maine to Connecticut from 1976 through 1993. After seven years in a variety of positions with major publishers in New York and San Francisco, he joined the American Booksellers Association in 2000, and currently serves as the Director of Book Sense Marketing. He is also on the Board of the Small Press Center, and has edited two volumes with Newmarket Press—*Book Sense Best Books* (2004) and *Book Sense Best Children's Books* (2005).

Nancy Olson has owned and operated Quail Ridge Books & Music in Raleigh, NC, since 1984, which has grown from 1,200 sq. ft. to 9,000+ sq. ft and sales of $3.2 million. The bookstore won three major awards in 2001: *Publishers Weekly* Bookseller of the Year, Charles Haslam Award for Excellence in Bookselling; Pannell Award for Excellence in Children's Bookselling. It was voted "Best in the Triangle" in the *Independent Weekly* and *Metro Magazine*.

Jill A. Tardiff is publishing industry consultant and project manager working under her banner company Bamboo River Associates. She is also advertising manager for such print and online publications as *Parabola—Tradition, Myth, and the Search for Meaning*, as well as contributing editor at *Publishers Weekly*. Jill is the past president of the Women's National Book Association (WNBA) and WNBA-New York City chapter, 2004–2006 and 2000–2005, respectively. She is currently WNBA's National Reading Group Month Committee Chair and Coordinator and its United Nations Department of Public Information NGO Chief Representative. She is currently working on several book proposals on modern-day pilgrimage.

RESOURCES

THE INTERNET

About reading groups and book clubs

■ **ReadingGroupChoices.com**—Over 600 guides available plus give-aways and fun and interactive materials for reading groups.

■ **bookgroupexpo.com**— Come to book group expo and celebrate.

■ **Book-Clubs-Resource.com**—A guide to book clubs and reading groups with a collection of links and information for readers, including information about saving with discount book clubs.

■ **BookClubCookbook.com**—Recipes and food for thought from your book club's favorite books and authors

About Books

■ **ShelfAwareness.com**—A free e-mail newsletter dedicated to helping the people in stores, in libraries and on the Web buy, sell, and lend books most wisely.

■ **PageByPageBooks.com**—Read classic books online for free.

■ **PublishingInsidertypad.com**—Books, music, movies, the big picture, and absurd rants.

■ **GenerousBooks.com**—A community for those who love books and love to discuss them

■ **BookMuse.com**— Commentary, author bios, and suggestions for further reading

■ **BookBrowse.com**— Book reviews, excerpts, and author interviews

■ **AverageReader.com**—Book reviews - honest and to the point

■ **BookSpot.com**—Help in your search for the best book-related content on the Web

■ **Publisher Web Sites**—Find additional topics for discussion, special offers for book groups, and other titles of interest.

Algonquin Books of Chapel Hill — **algonquin.com**

Appledore Books — **appledorebooks.com**

Atlantic Monthly Press — **groveatlantic.com**

Avon A – **avonbooks.com**

Ballantine Books — **ballantinebooks.com**

Broadway Books — **broadwaybooks.com**

Conari Press — **conari.com**

Doubleday — **doubleday.com**

Europa Editions — **EuropaEditions.com**

Forge — **tor-forge.com**

Free Press — **simonsays.com**

Graywolf Press — **graywolfpress.org**

Grove Press — **grovepress.com**

Harlequin — **eHarlequin.com**

Harper Paperbacks — **harpercollins.com**

Harper Perennial — **harperperennial.com**

Houghton Mifflin Harcourt — **houghtonmifflinbookscom.com**

Hyperion — **hyperionbooks.com**

Mariner Books — **marinerbooks.com**

Moody Publishers — **moodypublishers.com**

Penguin Books — **penguin.com**

Picador USA — **picadorusa.com**

Plume Books — **plumebooks.com**

PublicAffairs — **publicaffairsbooks.com**

Random House — **randomhouse.com**

Simon Spotlight Entertainment — **simonsays.com**

Soho Press — **sohopress.com**

Thomas Dunne Books — **thomasdunnebooks.com**

Tor — **tor-forge.com**

Unbridled Books — **unbridledbooks.com**

Vanguard Press — **vanguardpressbooks.com**

Vintage Books — **readinggroupcenter.com**

Voice — **everywomansvoice.com**

William Morrow — **williammorrow.com**

BOOKS

■ ***Book Lust: Recommended Reading for Every Mood, Moment, and Reason*** by Nancy Pearl
Published by Sasquatch Books, ISBN 1-57061-381-8, $16.95.

■ ***More Book Lust: Recommended Reading for Every Mood, Moment, and Reason*** by Nancy Pearl
Published by Sasquatch Books, ISBN 1-57061-435-0 $16.95.

■ ***The Book Club Companion: A Comprehensive Guide to the Reading Group Experience*** by Diana Loevy
Published by Berkeley Books, ISBN 0-425-21009-X, $14.00.

■ ***The Book Club Cookbook: Recipes and Food for Thought from Your Book Club's Favorite Books and Authors*** by Judy Gelman and Vicki Levy Krupp
Published by Tarcher/Penguin, ISBN 1-58542-322-X, $15.95.

■ ***The Book Group Book: A Thoughtful Guide to Forming and Enjoying a Stimulating Book Discussion Group.*** Edited by Ellen Slezak and Margaret Eleanor Atwood
Published by Chicago Review Press, ISBN 1-5565-2412-9, $14.95.

■ ***Circles of Sisterhood: A Book Discussion Group Guide for Women of Color*** by Pat Neblett
Published by Writers & Readers, ISBN 0-8631-6245-2, $14.

■ ***Family Book Sharing Groups: Start One in Your Neighborhood!*** by Marjorie R. Simic with Eleanor C. MacFarlane
Published by the Family Literacy Center
ISBN 1-8837-9011-5, $6.95.

■ ***Good Books Lately: The One-Stop Resource for Book Groups and Other Greedy Readers*** by Ellen Moore and Kira Stevens
Published by St. Martin's Griffin, ISBN 978-0-312-30961-9, $13.95.

■ ***Leave Me Alone, I'm Reading: Finding and Losing Myself in Books*** by Maureen Corrigan
Published by Random House, ISBN 0-375-50425-7, $24.95.

■ *Literature Circles: Voice and Choice in Book Clubs and Reading Groups* by Harvey Daniels
Published by Stenhouse Publishers
ISBN 1-5711-0333-3, $22.50.

■ *The Mother-Daughter Book Club: How Ten Busy Mothers and Daughters Came Together to Talk, Laugh and Learn Through Their Love of Reading* by Shireen Dodson and Teresa Barker
Published by HarperCollins, ISBN 0-0609-5242-3, $14.

■ *Running Book Discussion Groups* by Lauren Zina John
Published by Neal-Schuman, ISBN 1-55570-542-1.

■ *The Reading Group Handbook: Everything You Need to Know to Start Your Own Book Club* by Rachel Jacobsohn
Published by Hyperion, ISBN 0-786-88324-3, $12.95.

■ *Recipe for a Book Club: A Monthly Guide for Hosting Your Own Reading Group: Menus & Recipes, Featured Authors, Suggested Readings, and Topical Questions* by Mary O'Hare and Rose Storey
Published by Capital Books, ISBN 978-1-931-86883-9, $19.95

■ *Talking About Books: Literature Discussion Groups in K–8 Classrooms* by Kathy Short
Published by Heinemann, ISBN 0-3250-0073-5, $24.

■ *Thirteen Ways of Looking at the Novel* by Jane Smiley Published by Knopf, ISBN 1-4000-4059-0, $26.95.

■ *What to Read: The Essential Guide for Reading Group Members and Other Book Lovers (Revised)* by Mickey Pearlman
Published by HarperCollins, ISBN 0-0609-5313-6, $14.00.

■ *A Year of Reading: A Month-By-Month Guide to Classics and Crowd-Pleasers for You or Your Book Group* by H. E. Ellington and Jane Freimiller
Published by Sourcebooks, ISBN 1-5707-1935-7, $14.95.

WHAT'S IN A NAME?
Reading Groups Choose Creative Ways to Describe Themselves

It's not surprising that words are important to book group members. Readers marvel at their favorite authors' ability to put words together in a way that evokes deep emotions, both positive and negative. They appreciate and choose words for their meaning, of course, but also for their sound, their nuances, their derivations, and their double meanings. So it's probably not surprising that book groups put considerable effort and creativity into selecting the words to describe themselves. The names that they choose somehow reflect the character of the group as a whole, which may be quite different from the words that each member would choose to describe themselves.

Take, for example, the groups that obviously intensely enjoy the reading group experience. A sample of group names from *Reading Group Choices* subscribers include the **Better Than Therapy Book Club**; **Reading Between the Wines**; **Who Picked This Book? Club**; **Face2Face**; and **Boisterous Banter**.

Apparently, some groups just like to have fun – and that includes taking the time to name themselves. For example, there are the **Marmaladies**; the **Litwits**; the **Chapter Chicks**; the **Alleycats**; the **Bookworm Biddies**; the **Literal Hotties**; **Out on a Tangent**; the **Literary Lofty Dogs**; the **Happy Bookers**; **Girlz R Us**; the **Deadly Divas**; and the **Bemused Bibliophiles.**

And then there are the groups that take on their own identity. The names tell you a lot about the character of the group – the **Benson Bifocals**; **Book Broads and John**; the **Amigos & Flamingos Book Club**; **Soul Sistas**; the **Crazy Eight**; the **Eclectics**; **Soccer Moms Book Club**; and the **Renaissance Men's Book Club.**

Some groups express their appreciation for the written word in the name they choose, such as the **B.A.G. Ladies** (Books Are Good); and the **Rabid Readers.** And some actually play with words within their name, like the **Literary Locusts of Lochmere**; **WOW** (Women of Words); and **StatIS Quo.** Other groups apparently really like the reading experience, like the **Spine Crackers**; the **Joyful Page Turners**; and the **Cranial Crunch.**

A few groups are literally literary, like the **AlaKaye Literary Society**; the **Final Word Literary Guild**; the **Grand Dames of Literature**; **La Literati**—and *perhaps* **Barely Literate.**

But some groups leave no doubt what they are up to. Whether you approve or not, there are the **Bath Tub Readers**, for example, **Andy's Wives;** and the **Read Naked** groups. You can also guess what goes on during the gatherings at **Just Mai Tai'n**; **Literate Epicureans**; the **Martini Book Club**; **Mysteries on Main Street**; **Fiction Addiction**; and **Tea and Tales.**

Some groups may use their name to remind themselves of when or where they meet. For example, the **BLT Club's** expanded name is **Books Last Tuesday.** Then there is the **Gazebo Gathering**; **Booked for Lunch**; **MysticMommas**; and the **Rural Readers.** In some cases, though, the mnemonic device may lead to some confusion – consider for example **Reading in the Rafters**!

For those of you who may be forming new groups, perhaps there are some ideas here that can lead you to the perfect name. For those—and there are many, we're sure—who have other creative descriptive devices, please send them to us. We'll publish a few of them in an upcoming e-newsletter. In any case, thanks for keeping the joy of reading alive.

INDEX BY SUBJECT/INTEREST